0

EVIL
TWINS

EVIL
TWINS

EVIL TIMES TWO . . .

The Cookie Ladies—Dorthea Beck and her twin sister Mary lived and worked together until they retired in their late sixties. Known to most as the Cookie Ladies, who baked and gave away delicious chocolate-chip cookies, they shocked their quiet Illinois community when Dorthea turned on her sister in a violent rage and beat her to death with a walking cane.

Doctor, Doctor—Cyril and Stewart Marcus seemed to have it all. Handsome successful twin gynecologists, they were the talk of New York medical circles. But their growing addiction to painkillers, amphetamines, and barbiturates began to consume them, jeopardize the lives of their patients, and ultimately, result in their own untimely deaths.

Twisted Sister—At one time, Sunny and Gina Han, strikingly beautiful 23-year-old South Korean-born identical twins, had been inseparable. But when Sunny turned her sister in to the police for stealing, Gina spent six months in jail—allegedly plotting to kill her once-beloved twin sister.

LOOK INSIDE FOR MORE
CHILLING TRUE STORIES OF

EVIL TWINS

*St. Martin's Press titles
by John Glatt*

FOR I HAVE SINNED
EVIL TWINS

EVIL TWINS

John Glatt

St. Martin's Press

To Audrey and Mavis Hirschberg: my own identical twin cousins.

CONTENTS

AUTHOR'S NOTE

The stories of all these twins are one hundred percent true. Although they are based on actual cases, names and characteristics of certain minor players and innocent victims depicted in this book have been changed.

FOREWORD

Twins exert a unique fascination. From the very beginning, in their mother's womb, twins are connected by a deep bond that survives even years-long separation and usually remains intact until death. So connected are some twins that they even appear to share a single personality and can communicate without speech.

Obviously twins have a very special relationship with one another which is generally very close, with ups and downs like any normal family. Psychologists, anthropologists and sociologists have studied twins for years, discovering many intriguing but harmless patterns of behavior. However, no phenomenon is more complex or bizarre than when twins commit murder.

When twins kill together—using the force of their bond in such a diabolical way—an unparalleled instrument of evil is unleashed. Even more bizarre is when an inexplicable split occurs, and one twin murderously turns on the other.

It is almost beyond comprehension to imagine that there can be evil dead ringers—but there are. Although cases of evil twins are very rare in the annals of criminology they do occur and are usually far more mysterious and complex than other cases of routine homicide.

Scientists believe human genetics dictate behaviors as diverse as smoking, career choices and marriage. But do they also predetermine who will become a murderer?

In *Evil Twins* I have collected twelve cases of twins who have committed terrible sins with, or against each other. The seeds of their destruction often date back to the womb when some mysterious force of nature, binding the twins together, became infected and turned bad.

Identical twins share the closest possible human relationship—they are exact clones with the same genetic composition—so the thought of one identical twin murdering another almost defies belief.

Such was the case of Jeff and Greg Henry, identical twins who evolved a bizarre master–slave relationship. After years of ridicule and torture, Jeff finally put an end to their twinship with a single shotgun blast.

Tim and Todd Nicholson were bitter rivals in love and business, with one twin always trying to outdo the other. Tim would ultimately win the dangerous game, after killing his twin and then marrying his dead brother's fiancée when he came out of prison.

The intriguing question of whether twins develop similar habits and characteristics by nature or nurture has puzzled scientists for generations. Jane and Jean Hopkins, who made history by becoming the first twins to try to murder their own children, are a macabre example of why this question remains so difficult to answer. Gifted with beauty and brains, the twins from Van Buren, Arkansas, seemed to have the world at their feet. But ultimately, in their mid-thirties, they would both fall tragic victim to the same mental illness, which would lead to bloody murder.

The special tie between twins is often closer than any other relationship in life, including the maternal. When Gretchen Graham stood by and watched her four-year-old son Shawn perish in a fire, without raising a finger to save him, her twin sister Gloria was with her every evil step of the way.

A common thread of all these cases is the strange, almost unearthly power that twins can exert over each other. Both brilliant gynecologists, Doctors Cyril and Stewart Marcus were at the cutting edge of the medical establishment. After publishing a well-received book on breakthrough infertility techniques, the twin doctors were hailed as brilliant. But Cyril led his brother down the nightmarish path of drug addiction. The wealthy doctors lost everything and hit rock bottom, before dying together in their posh Manhattan apartment as they tried to kick their habits.

Betty Wilson also experimented with drugs before marrying wealthy eye doctor Jack Wilson, who was her ticket to the good life. But when she tired of the millionaire doctor, police claimed, she enlisted her twin Peggy's help to find a hit man to murder him, so she could inherit his millions.

Many of the cases I present are highly disturbing, as they offer a unique insight into the human psyche, forcing us to question our own relationships in life.

Dorthea and Mary Beck never left each other's side for sixty-eight years. The inseparable elderly spinsters seemed like a devoted married couple and were beloved as kindly eccentrics in the small Illinois town they lived in all their life. But when one of the twins became sick, refusing to eat or take her medication, her sister exacted a terrible revenge by beating her to death for threatening to leave her.

Even well-seasoned Orange County detectives couldn't believe the cold, calculating manner in which Gina Han recruited two teenage boys to help her kill her identical twin sister Sunny. The beautiful twenty-three-year-old Korean immigrant would have succeeded but for Sunny's quick thinking, which led to Gina's capture and ultimate conviction for attempted murder.

No single woman in Los Angeles was safe from the date-rape reign of terror unleashed by handsome twins George and Stefan Spitzer. After failing to break into the movie business in Hollywood, the sexually perverted twins embarked on a fifteen-year career of drugging beautiful young women, raping them and then videotaping their depravities.

During the course of my research for *Evil Twins*, I have interviewed countless people, too numerous to name. I am indebted to the district attorneys, homicide detectives, twin experts, journalists and family members of both victims and murderers who have so generously aided me in this project. I must also thank convicted killer Tim Nicholson for talking to me about his case and sharing his insight into his motivations.

For my background research I have used newspapers and magazine reports as well as previously unpublished police reports and court records. The conclusions that I reach and the descriptions of the crimes are drawn from scores of personal interviews and my extensive research.

A special thanks must go to Professor Robert McCree, Associate Professor for Security Management at John Jay College of Criminal Justice in Manhattan, for allowing me full access to the college criminal library. I am also indebted to Detective Chris Helgert for his invaluable help and background in "The Twins From Hell."

I would also like to thank Wensley Clarkson, Charlie Spicer, Peter Miller, Dorsey Mills, Delin Cormeny, David Hayes, Aryn Stapp, Annette Witheridge, Susan Chenery, Chris Wilson, Chris Bowen, Fred and Linda Wehner, Daphna Inbar, Roger Hitts, Peter Williams, and Anthony Hayden-Guest.

EVIL
TWINS

One

SEPARATED BY MURDER

One brother was a saint but his identical twin was a sinner. Yet Greg and Jeff Henry were inseparable—locked together in a sado-masochistic relationship that would end in a grisly death.

It is a twisted tale of a strange, dysfunctional Southern family that could have come straight out of the pages of an Erskine Caldwell novel.

Throughout their lives Greg delighted in intimidating and terrorizing his meeker brother, ordering him to fetch beer after beer and then clean up. To reinforce his dominance, Greg often fired his .22 caliber rifle at Jeff to scare him, spraying their apartment walls with bullet holes.

The Henry brothers lived and worked together in a strange master–slave relationship for nearly thirty-seven years, until they were ripped apart by a single shotgun blast at their home in rural Georgia.

Killed instantly was Greg, the brutal power monger, who finally pushed things too far one night after a marathon drinking session, when he threatened Jeff with a shotgun. For once the docile brother turned, savagely killing his twin before giving himself up to the police and being charged with murder.

Even as babies, Greg and Jeff Henry faced an uphill battle for survival in a world they could never quite come to terms with. They were born on January 23, 1955, in Dublin, Georgia, during a freak snowstorm. It became a family joke that the real reason the town's antiquated switchboard broke down from too many calls wasn't the snow, but the arrival of the Henry twins.

Their father, Dick Henry, was a successful executive, managing a local chemical plant, and their mother, Sue, once the most beautiful girl in Dublin, had won many local beauty contests in her youth.

Dick and Sue, who already had two boys, were overjoyed when the twins were born after a difficult Cesarean section. But within a few months Greg became sick and almost died. He was diagnosed with a brain disorder and had to have his spine tapped to save his life.

As infants, the Henry twins captured the imagination of the town. Sue, then thirty-six, would proudly push them through the streets to church every Sunday in their double stroller. And they caused quite a stir at Dick's country club, where they would play with their two older brothers, Chris and Mike.

From the very beginning they were known as "the twins" and never referred to by their names. Even their mother couldn't tell them apart and would ask them to raise their shirts to identify them, as one had an inner belly-button and the other, an outer.

Sue Henry dressed them alike in fabulous no-expense-spared outfits and the twins became her pride and joy. She spoiled them rotten. As infants Jeff and Greg were inseparable and even sucked each other's thumbs. They played together and slept together and seemed like a single person inhabiting two identical bodies.

"If you had one, you had them both," declared their mother. "I don't remember them being any different."

Even before they could talk English they had instinctively developed their own language, which no one else could understand. They would happily jabber away for hours, using strange words like "Jogabawamama" and "Debogdoogwotama."

But the Henrys' perfect world fell apart when, in April 1958, Dick was diagnosed with brain cancer and died a year later. While he was on his deathbed, Sue brought Greg and Jeff into the hospital to say their final good-byes.

"Aren't they adorable?" said their dying father as he kissed them for the last time.

So at the age of forty, Sue—or Ma, as the twins called her—found herself a widow with just a small trust fund to support the twins and their two brothers.

"I'm a survivor," says the tough Southern belle, who became a secretary to make ends meet. "You do what you have to do to get by."

There seemed to be an almost supernatural, psychic bond between Jeff and Greg as they grew up. At the age of five Greg disappeared and couldn't be found anywhere. When Jeff was asked where his brother was hiding he immediately walked off and found him a mile away from their home. Somehow he was just drawn toward him.

Together the twins created their own world of fantasy and didn't seem to need anyone else. But from their earliest days Greg appeared to dominate Jeff, assuming the role of leader in all their games. By the time they started at a private pre-school and kindergarten, Jeff cheerfully took a back seat to his more extroverted brother, who always got better grades and made more friends. And wherever Greg led, Jeff followed.

From a young age the twins discovered a fascination for electrical appliances. When they were seven they surprised their mother by completely rewiring their bedroom, connecting every appliance to a single master switch so they could turn on everything at once.

It inspired them to want to become inventors when they grew up and they started reading everything they could about technology.

In 1962, Ma Henry remarried a local man

named Jack Wright. The seven-year-old twins hated their new stepfather, a strict disciplinarian who tried to rein them in. Jeff and Greg considered him physically abusive and would avoid him at all costs.

At home there were frequent arguments and fights between their mother and new stepfather, who did not get along. Ma Henry turned to drink to overcome her problems, finally divorcing Wright in 1973.

Painfully shy and far slower than his smarter brother, Jeff struggled through Henderson High School as a ''C''- and ''D''-grade student. The introverted Jeff was physically frail and far weaker than Greg, and developed an inferiority complex after failing to have his brother's success with the girls.

Jeff could barely read or write, but he found that he had a talent for fixing radios and stereos, spending hours happily tinkering away with the electronic devices. The tall, skinny teenager, who sported long, blond hair, dreamed of inventing revolutionary machines that would change the world, like the ones he read about in science fiction comics.

Though they looked alike, the twins were as different as chalk and cheese. Unlike his nervous brother, Greg was a fearless daredevil. He loved racing his bicycle up and down the hallway of his high school, showing off to the other kids with his patented wheelies.

During their late teens the twins fought over

everything and had an increasingly troubled relationship. Greg seemed to enjoy humiliating
his shy brother in public, ridiculing his whim-
sical ideas. But if Jeff ever dared to stand up
for himself and criticize Greg, it always ended
in a fight.

"They were going through that rebellion
thing," their mother would later explain.

The Henry family was torn apart when the
twins' eldest brother Richard was diagnosed
with schizophrenia and hospitalized in the late
1960s. It had a profound effect on Jeff who began to fear insanity might run in the family.

At the age of eighteen the twins graduated
high school, finding jobs in the mailroom of a
local company. Now that they were financially
sufficient they left home to get an apartment
together.

Both standing six foot two inches and weigh-
ing just one hundred and sixty pounds, the
wavy-haired, pencil-thin Henry twins were an
imposing sight. Their fellow workers found it
almost impossible to tell them apart, before getting to know them. Then it was easy to pick
out Greg by his loud bullying ways as opposed
to his quieter, more easy-going twin brother.

"We used to kid him and call him a little
wimp," said Ma. "He was so passive."

Two years after leaving high school, the twins
were briefly separated for the only time in their
life when Greg married his girlfriend, Julie.

Jeff, who had never had a girlfriend of his own, couldn't bear to be apart from Greg and moved into the basement of the house the couple bought. But the marriage was short-lived and Jeff was overjoyed when Julie left and the twins were reunited.

Taking a large apartment on Seville Drive in Clarkston, Georgia, Jeff and Greg decided to become rock stars. Greg bought a set of drums and Jeff tried to teach himself bass. They recruited a couple of friends to join their band, rehearsing late into the night in the basement of their new apartment.

During band practices Jeff and Greg would down cases of Budweiser beer until they could hardly stand up. And the more beer Greg drank, the meaner he became to Jeff.

Friend and fellow band member and Jason Hill remembers Greg Henry constantly picking fights with his weaker twin brother.

"When they weren't drinking they were pretty much normal," said Hill. "But when they started drinking—I don't mean a twelve-pack of beer but two or three cases—Greg turned into a different person."

The brothers were so proud of their drinking that they would save each empty beer case to stack up against the wall as trophies. And they delighted in proudly showing off their collection of empty beer "suitcases" that soon reached to the ceiling.

Fueled by beer, Greg would pound his drums

late into the night, refusing to allow the other band members to go home. On one occasion when Hill insisted on leaving at 2 a.m. so he could go to work the following morning, Greg flew into a rage, kicking his drum set across the floor.

"As we left you could hear Greg screaming at Jeff to carry on playing," remembered Hill. "You would have to drag him off those drums to stop him."

Greg Henry was often totally out of control, exploding at the slightest provocation. One night when the twins were staying with their mother, they started arguing so loudly that she asked them to be quiet.

"Greg gave me some lip," said Ma Henry. "And I don't take lip off my sons. When I told him not to talk to me like that he picked up a clock radio and hurled it across the room and it broke. Then he just grabbed his stuff and got into his car and left."

The growing tension between the twins escalated dramatically when they developed a fascination with firearms. They each bought themselves shotguns and proudly displayed them against the living room wall.

Now Greg's anger took on a sinister dimension. To make a point in an argument with Jeff, he would suddenly grab his .22-caliber firearm and start shooting up the room in fury.

Early one Sunday morning Jeff arrived at Jason Hill's apartment shaking with terror. He said he'd had enough of Greg and was moving out of their apartment.

"Greg had pulled a gun on him," remembered Hill. "Jeff wanted to get away from him and I don't blame him."

Although Jeff moved back with his mother, within a few weeks he found he couldn't bear to be separated from his twin brother. But as they moved into a new apartment together, Greg stepped up his reign of terror, making life even more miserable for the unfortunate Jeff.

The twins settled into a one-bedroom apartment at Tree Terrace in Maxham Road, Lithia Springs, and started drinking themselves into oblivion. Greg set up his drum kit in the front room and played along to his favorite rock 'n' roll albums into the early hours. He picked constant fights with Jeff, firing his gun indiscriminately at the least provocation.

In early 1989, Ma Henry, then seventy, decided to step in and try to get her twin sons' lives back on track. She was particularly concerned about Greg's drinking and the danger he posed to Jeff.

The twins had recently been arrested for driving under the influence and feared losing their licenses and not being able to drive their jointly owned Camaro sports car. So under pressure from Ma Henry they agreed to go on the wagon and give up alcohol.

The effects were immediate and they calmed

down and began to get along with each other
for the first time in many years. Turning over a
new leaf, they both found jobs as audio repair-
men at the Circuit City electronics store in
nearby Austell, Georgia.

At first the twins impressed their boss with
their enthusiasm and punctuality. They would
spend hours in the back room, tinkering around
with the broken amplifiers and televisions, as a
nonstop talk radio station played in the background. It was piece-work, and Jeff and Greg
took so long on repairs that they did not make
much money.

"They'd test it and test it," remembers their
Circuit City co-worker Ted Crowder. "They'd
help you for two hours and speak to you, while
neglecting their own work."

A few months into the job the brothers
started drinking again. While on the wagon
Greg had become addicted to coffee for the caf-
feine buzz. He drank so many cups a day that
he became sick. When a doctor friend suggested an occasional beer instead, saying it
would be harmless, Greg leapt at the chance.
Soon he was back to beer, drinking more heavily than ever, with Jeff following in his wake.

As the twins fell back into their drunken
ways, their fellow workers noticed Jeff becoming more and more paranoid and withdrawn. He
bit his fingernails to the quick and was always
scared that he was in trouble.

"Jeff had become like a Chihuahua," says Crowder. "He was real nervous."

At home the twins' relationship had deteriorated even further. The domineering Greg mentally tortured Jeff as they drank their way through cases of Budweiser every night. When Ma Henry visited her sons' apartment, she was horrified to see the stacks of empty beer containers piled up in rows against the wall.

"I knew they had a problem," she would later tell police. "[I] just didn't seem to be able to convince them that they did."

Things got so bad that Ma begged them to take the twelve-step program at Alcoholics Anonymous, but they refused, claiming that they were fine.

"I had discussed it with friends of mine that were friends of A.A.," said Ma Henry. "I was told that sometimes people had to get really violent before they recognized there was a problem. They had performed so well as children and had such a good reputation in their profession, that I couldn't convince them that they [needed help]."

Jeff began to confide in his mother about Greg's violent temper tantrums. He said he was frightened when his brother turned on him and began blasting off the shotgun that he kept by his bed.

When Ma challenged Greg, he admitted shooting at his twin once during a heated argument. But he apologized, saying that he had learned his lesson and would never do it again.

"Jeff was scared to death of Greg," said their mother. "He couldn't go to the bathroom without asking Greg's permission."

Since Greg's divorce almost fifteen years earlier, the twins had not dated, preferring their own company. But when a persistent young woman began pursuing Greg romantically, he told her that he was not interested. When she refused to take no for an answer he pulled out his shotgun and fired over her head, and she fled the apartment in fear for her life.

One Christmas in the late 1980s, Ma Henry organized a family reunion at her luxurious new home in Roswell, Georgia. After a full turkey dinner with all the trimmings, the twins and their brothers staged an impromptu musical jam while Ma washed the dishes.

Remembered Ma Henry: "Mike was there with his guitar and Greg had his guns [by his drum kit]. I was putting up with it because it was Christmas, but at two in the morning Jeff and Mike were ready to go to bed. And we went out to try and get Greg to go to bed but he just would not give up. He just sat there beatin' that drum. And he got mad."

Eventually, Greg drunkenly kicked his drums over and stormed into the house in a black mood. He went upstairs and climbed out of a second-floor bedroom window, sliding down the roof and landing in the garden.

When Ma heard Greg drunkenly staggering around outside, she went out in the garden in her pajamas to see if he was all right. It was a freezing night and when she failed to find Greg she gave up and went back to bed.

Half an hour later she was awakened by screams coming from the garden. Greg had fallen into a bed of roses and scratched himself badly. Staggering back into the house, he began hammering on his mother's bedroom door in tears.

"I let him in," said Ma, who felt sorry for him. "And he got into bed with me. He was just convulsing with crying. And he said, 'I almost blew it, didn't I?' I said [he had] and told him I loved him."

Then her weeping thirty-four-year-old son fell asleep in her arms until he woke up the next morning with a savage hangover.

In June 1990, the Circuit City store laid off most of their workforce because of a recession, but the Henry twins managed to stay on. Their supervisor liked their work, considering them hard workers and the two best technicians on his staff.

Although they were both drinking heavily, they still managed to get in on time, insisting on working longer hours than anyone else.

That Thanksgiving, Greg caught flu and went into work while the rest of the family celebrated at Ma's house. He spent the whole three-day holiday alone in the repair shop, catching up on his workload.

Over the next few months Jeff withdrew even further as his twin brother became ever-harder to live with. Jeff was now expected to be at Greg's constant beck and call, serving him beer after beer and preparing all the meals. And the more Greg demanded, the harder Jeff served his unappreciative brother. He would even politely thank him afterward.

"Jeff says thank you all the time," said Ma Henry. " 'Yes, ma'am, no, ma'am.' We used to say, 'Jeff, you could get run over by a Mack truck and you would get up and thank the man for not killing you.''

But alcohol was taking its toll on the twins. They worked during the day and drank in the evenings and on weekends, staying in their one-bedroom apartment watching football games and old movies. Every night Greg would play his drums into the early hours and the neighbors were beginning to complain about the noise and the twins' constant arguments.

Late one night in June 1991, the apartments' security officer, W. M. Montgomery, was summoned after Greg and Jeff got into a violent argument. When he entered the apartment he was shocked to see them blind drunk and covered in blood, the apartment littered with empty beer cans.

"Greg had a cut hand and Jeff had blood on his shirt," remembered Montgomery. "There was blood on the carpet and the Sheetrock wall opposite the doorway was damaged.''

The twins refused to discuss why they were arguing, and when Montgomery walked through the squalid apartment, he saw Greg's loaded .12-gauge pump shotgun with pistol grips lying on a bed. When the guard asked them if they were on drugs, the twins angrily denied it, ordering him to leave.

On his way out, Montgomery told them that he would be reporting the incident to the landlord and they would be evicted. Then Greg burst into a rage, slamming the door as hard as he could behind Montgomery.

A few days later Greg and Jeff received a landlord's eviction letter, ordering them out by the end of the month. They were told they were breaking their lease as there were two people occupying a one-bedroom apartment.

The first thing the twins did after receiving the letter was to call their mother for help. Immediately the indomitable seventy-two-year-old Henry matriarch came to their rescue, as she always did. Telling her sons not to worry, she found them a two-bedroom apartment across the road in Sweetwater Creek, even helping them move in the following weekend.

After moving out the furniture, Greg told Jeff to go back and clean up. While Greg spent the rest of the afternoon watching a football game, Jeff dutifully scrubbed the blood off the carpet and threw out hundreds of empty beer cans.

*   *   *

On Sunday, December 15, Greg and Jeff awoke at noon to spend the day drinking and watching a football double-header on television. Over the last month, the brothers had been drinking harder than ever and it was beginning to affect their work.

Three weeks earlier, Jeff's Circuit City boss had sent him home for being drunk, giving him an official warning. Ever sensitive, Jeff had sunk into a depression, fearing that his job was now in jeopardy and he would soon be unemployed.

After getting up late, the brothers settled down on the settee, wearing identical white T-shirts and faded jeans, to watch the first Falcons game. They began knocking back Budweisers as they argued about the finer points of the game.

By late afternoon, between games, Greg ordered Jeff to the kitchen to prepare him a meal of shrimp and fried potatoes and bring more beer. They were already drunk as they ate together and began watching the second football game. When it was over they watched a couple of movies on their betamax recorder, chugging back beer after beer.

It was one a.m. when they turned off the television and began debating Jeff's fanciful new theory for a revolutionary source of power. Through a haze of alcohol, Jeff enthusiastically explained that the power would be 99 percent efficient and pollution-free. Greg started laughing at him, calling him a dumb-ass imbecile and a moron.

When Jeff told his brother that he had a right to his theory, Greg turned violent, viciously lashing out at his twin.

"[He started] hitting me and cursing me," Jeff would later testify. "He knocked me out of my chair to the floor and pulled me up by the hair."

Greg suddenly ran to his bedroom, and Jeff's first thought was that he was going for the loaded shotgun that he always kept by the bed. Fearing for his life, Jeff ran into the other bedroom to get his own gun to defend himself.

Jeff felt a rush of adrenaline as he rushed toward Greg's room, smashing the door open with the barrel of his gun. Inside, Greg was lying flat out on the bed, drunk.

All Jeff's years of ridicule and torment suddenly came to a head as the twins had their final confrontation.

Their eyes met briefly as everything seemed to go into slow motion. Jeff screamed out, "Take this!" shooting his brother in the chest at point-blank range. Greg stared at Jeff in stunned disbelief as his chest exploded, his lungs splattering out over the bedroom wall. On hearing the shotgun blast and seeing the flash, Jeff went into shock. Then his nightmare began. He couldn't believe that he had actually pulled the trigger on his brother. He felt himself being

separated and torn in two. It was as if the shotgun blast had ripped his very molecules apart.
He knew he would never be the same again.

Then he dashed out of the bedroom and into
the hall to try and calm down, as the full horror
of what he had done sank in.

"I threw my gun away and went back in,"
he would tell homicide detectives several hours
later. "I saw Greg lying on the bed."

In a mad moment of desperation, Jeff
screamed as he jumped on top of his dying
brother, begging him not to die and leave him
alone. He used his palm to try and stem the
bright red blood oozing from the wound, but it
was too late. Greg died in his twin brother's
arms, with one blazing eye still open.

"I started screaming and yelling," said Jeff.
"I saw he was wounded and I shook him and
tore open his shirt."

In a frantic attempt to bring him back to life,
Jeff began giving Greg mouth-to-mouth resus-
citation. For five long, agonizing minutes he
tried unsuccessfully to breathe life back into his
twin.

With tears running down his face into his
brother's blood, Jeff looked at his brother's one
gazing eye; a demented stare that would haunt
him forever. Finally he couldn't take it anymore
and closed the eye, screamed and ran barefoot
out of the apartment.

Jumping in his car, Jeff drove off to find a
pay phone to call his mother for help. It was

two in the morning and Ma Henry was asleep when the telephone by her bed started ringing. When it wouldn't stop she picked it up to receive the shocking news.

But, though Ma Henry had managed to rescue her son from schoolboy scrapes to unemployment, poverty and eviction in the past, murder was something she would not be able to save him from.

"Mom, my God, my God, I've killed Greg," sobbed her tearful son into the phone at a nearby Citgo gas station.

Oblivious to the freezing temperatures, he stood under a streetlight covered in his brother's blood and tearfully told Ma Henry what had happened.

"I tried to revive him, Ma," he cried. "I gave him CPR, Ma. I did everything I could. He's dead, Ma, he's dead."

Remaining calm, Ma asked him if he was certain his brother was dead. When Jeff said that he was, Ma told him to stay put while she called the police. She promised that she would then come and meet him at the filling station and look after him.

After reassuring him that everything would be all right, she put down the phone and called the police.

Later, Ma would admit that she was not surprised about what had happened; in fact, she had even been expecting it.

"There you go—I knew this would happen," she would say philosophically.

At 2:31 a.m. Douglas County Police Officer Mike Hicks drove into the Citgo station and found Jeff Henry waiting by the pay phone. His white T-shirt and faded blue jeans were covered in blood and he had a grotesque reddish-brown circle around his mouth, making him resemble a circus clown. With his hand on his gun, Hicks approached Jeff and asked him what had happened.

"I killed my brother," he sobbed. "It was self-defense. He had a rifle and he shot at me so I shot him with a shotgun."

Hicks could smell the alcohol on Jeff's breath as he handcuffed and searched him. Then he asked Jeff to get into the police car and direct him to his Sweetwater Creek apartment to find Greg. Shaking with terror, Jeff said that he would do anything to help.

During the short drive, Officer Hicks radioed for back-up and they were met outside the apartment by Lieutenant Eddie Morris. Hicks stayed in the police car with Jeff while Lieutenant Morris went into the Henry brothers' apartment to investigate.

Carefully threading his way through the scores of empty beer cans littering the front room, Morris entered the bedroom to find Greg's body lying on the bed next to his Rutger .22 shotgun. He was stripped to the waist and

Morris could see the gaping gunshot wound in his chest. When he failed to get a pulse and found no signs of breathing, he radioed headquarters that they had a probable homicide on their hands.

Checking the rest of the apartment, Morris saw Jeff's recently fired shotgun lying on the bed in the other bedroom and found a spent shell on the bathroom floor. He also noticed a large hole in Greg's bedroom door caused by Jeff's shotgun barrel.

Back at the station, Jeff was read his Miranda rights and arrested for the murder of his twin brother. He immediately confessed to killing Greg, telling detectives that it was self-defense after Greg had shot at him four times.

In a videotaped confession after the arrest, Jeff claimed he hadn't known his Mossberg shotgun was loaded and that he was merely trying to frighten Greg. As the video camera rolled, Jeff sat bowed over a long Formica table as he kept staring at his still-bloody hands in total disbelief.

"I just killed my twin brother," he sobbed nervously. "Look at me! I have my brother's blood all over me."

Although Jeff swore he was telling the "honest truth," when detectives later examined Greg's blood-soaked semi-automatic rifle, they found no bullets in the chamber and determined that it had not been fired.

"He shot at me four times," Jeff still insisted. "He's done that in the past. This time I just clicked. I showed him my gun—boastfully—and basically I just shot him accidentally. I honestly didn't know the gun was loaded."

At 5:35 a.m. Ma Henry and her second-eldest son Mike backed up Jeff's story, telling homicide detectives about the twins' violent relationship. Both expressed amazement that the victimized Jeff had killed his bullying twin and not the other way around.

They said that Greg had often fired at his twin brother in anger and his uncontrollable temper was exacerbated by heavy drinking. But they explained that although Greg ill-treated Jeff, the twins were completely dependent on each other.

"They were so close," Ma told police. "They were just like one person speaking to you. I've lost two sons, for the time being. I want one of them back."

As he awaited his murder trial in Douglas County Jail, Jeff's lawyers prepared to use the "battered wife syndrome" as his main line of defense. This was the first time this defense would be used in Georgia in a case not involving a husband and wife, and it set such a precedent that it would take years to bring the case to trial.

Devastated by the family murder, Ma Henry found herself in an impossible, heartbreaking situation as she stood squarely behind Jeff, defending him against his dead twin. She even came to court offering to put up her home as surety to bail Jeff out of prison until his trial, but was turned down by a judge.

"I'm the victim's mother and the defendant's mother," she told reporters. "I'm caught in the middle. All I can do is stand behind my one son and support him."

And at Greg's funeral she urged family and friends to say a prayer for Jeff, saying that he needed all the help he could get.

In the months after Greg's murder a team of psychiatrists and experts visited Douglas County Jail to examine Jeff and determine his state of mind. Psychologist Dr. Dennis L. Herendeen met Jeff for a series of interviews in the visitors' room in the jail house. Throughout the sessions Jeff fidgeted, appearing defensive in his answers.

Saying that he experienced deep feelings of guilt about Greg's death, Jeff told doctors that he had fallen into a depression since the killing. He said he feared having a nervous breakdown and had suffered severe anxiety attacks and nervous rashes in jail and couldn't sleep.

"I'm badly in need of a vacation," he told Dr. Herendeen.

Tests showed that Jeff had below-average intelligence with an IQ level of just seventy-five.

"He is a warm, quiet individual who is fairly

eager to please,'' wrote Dr. Herendeen in his report to the court.

Jeff opened up to Dr. Herendeen, admitting being shy and having an inferiority complex. He described his relationship with Greg as ''troubled,'' saying that he had turned to religion and looked for God's forgiveness.

''[Jeff] appears extremely dependent and submissive,'' wrote Dr. Herendeen. ''He passively allows others to assume responsibility for major areas of his life because of an extreme desire to please them and inability to function independently.''

The psychologist found that Jeff had little self-direction, looking to Greg for a sense of identity and purpose. He had built up his twin brother as the stronger, smarter, more competent one, seeking his protection and shelter from the hardships of life. Rather than running the risk of being alone, Jeff had eagerly allowed Greg to enslave him and become his master.

''He may allow himself to be intimidated and abused rather than assert himself for fear of being even worse off alone,'' wrote Dr. Herendeen.

It took almost three-and-a-half years for Jeff to go on trial for his brother's murder. During the long months in jail Jeff read comics and prayed, desperately trying to come to terms with killing his brother. Ma Henry visited him every week without fail, trying to bolster his sagging morale as he slowly became acclimated to institutionalization.

He had constant nightmares and the only peace he found was when he dreamed of Greg and the good times they had once had as children.

"We play together and we have so much fun," he would recall, a rare smile coming to his thin, bony face. "Those are the only good dreams I have, because we're together again."

On Monday, April 17, 1995, soon after his fortieth birthday, Jeff Henry arrived in court in heavy shackles to defend himself against the charge of murdering his twin brother. One of his attorneys, Bruce Harvey, had spent three years preparing the defense, which was a twist on the battered-wife syndrome.

"It isn't just women who are battered," explained Harvey before the trial began. "There are siblings."

He brought in a clinical social worker, who was an expert on emotional abuse, to testify that Jeff suffered from battered-wife syndrome and post-traumatic stress disorder.

But prosecutor Beau McClain disagreed, saying it was a clear-cut case of murder.

"The question is not whether Greg Henry deserved what he got or even if he brought it on himself," said McClain. "The question is whether Jeff Henry had a legal right to take his brother's life."

McClain told the jury that Greg was killed in a "drunken fury," pointing out that Greg's shotgun had never been fired, as Jeff still claimed.

In a moment of high drama, the Henry matriarch defiantly took the stand to defend one twin son against the other. Wearing a pink jacket and constantly dabbing her eyes with a handkerchief, Ma carfully told the court how Greg could become a monster, saying even she had been scared of his vicious temper.

"Greg would normally be just as sweet and kind as Jeff," she sobbed. "But when he would reach a certain point in his [beer] consumption, he would just get ballistic."

She recounted a night when he had gotten drunk at her house and she'd implored him not to drive home until he had sobered up.

"He got up from the recliner and he pushed me," she recounted. "And he said, 'Get out of my way, I'm going.' Well Greg had never hit me before."

Then she spoke about the strange, tortured relationship her sons had had since childhood.

"They loved each other more than any kind of love I've ever seen," said Ma. "It was like one identity in two bodies."

It was riveting testimony and when Ma came off the stand, one of the defense lawyers told her it was one of the best courtroom performances he had ever witnessed.

The emotionally charged trial sent tempers

boiling over on both sides. Bruce Harvey was even jailed twice by the judge for contempt of court after losing his temper.

The three-week trial ended in a hung jury and was finally declared a mistrial. Half the jury held out for acquittal, publicly declaring that Jeff should be released so he wouldn't have to go through another trial.

A month later Jeff Henry returned to Douglas County Court to request bail so he could live with his mother until his second trial. To focus attention on her son's plight, Ma organized a rally on the courthouse lawn for thirty friends and family. She tied yellow ribbons around the trees and made placards, demanding Jeff's release.

With heavy coverage of his first trial in the local newspaper, there was great sympathy for Jeff in the community. And during the lunchtime recess his supporters gathered on the lawn outside the courthouse where a picnic of barbecue sandwiches and deviled eggs was served under an oak tree bedecked in yellow ribbons.

Ma Henry and Jeff were totally unaware that prosecutors and the defense were spending their lunch time at a secret meeting to hammer out a plea bargain. And as they agreed that, if Jeff would plead guilty to voluntary manslaughter to be freed on time served, Ma Henry was running through the court building, searching for the defense team.

"Where's the attorney?" she cried. "What is going on?"

When court resumed after lunch a shackled Jeff stood arm-in-arm with his mother before Judge Robert James, still hoping for bail.

The judge, who had watched the picnic outside with disapproval, told Ma that it harked back to an era when trials drew entertainment-hungry crowds.

Jeff's face visibly dropped as he gripped Ma Henry's arm even tighter, convinced that he would now have to spend many more months behind bars until his new trial date.

And it wasn't until the judge patiently explained the plea-bargain deal that it dawned on the Henrys that Jeff would be free immediately if he pleaded guilty to the lesser charge.

Jeff instantly agreed and was sentenced to ten years, then released on time served. But Judge James gave him a stern warning to stay away from any alcohol or face a new jail term.

Five minutes later Jeff hesitantly walked out of the courtroom looking bewildered, clutching an orange garbage bag with his belongings in his right hand. Alongside was his jubilant mother, triumphantly tossing roses to her cheering supporters.

A flock of reporters descended on the courtroom steps as Jeff savored his first breath of freedom since the night of Greg's death. Dorothy Smith, one of the jurors convinced of his innocence in his first trial, rushed up the steps to hug him, boasting that she had been one of those to force the mistrial.

Jeff blinked nervously as his tired, greenish-blue eyes adapted to the bright sunlight and flashing cameras, and he tried to express his emotions to the press.

''I'm going to start all over,'' he said. Suddenly Ma Henry was overcome by the emotion of the moment and burst into tears.

''You're the best mother in the world,'' Jeff told her, hugging her tightly. ''My mother and my family got me through this.''

Although Jeff might have been legally free, he was still imprisoned by nightmarish memories of the night that he killed Greg. He moved into his mother's Roswell house and tried to adapt to the outside world, but without Greg his life would never be the same.

In the four years since the trial, hardly an hour goes by when Jeff doesn't think about his dead twin.

Ma Henry, now a feisty seventy-nine years old, takes care of him, but he rarely leaves her house as he suffers from agoraphobia—a fear of open spaces. He hardly eats Ma's home cooking, which he—and Greg—once enthusiastically devoured. He has lost sixty pounds and his tall, thin body is emaciated. He no longer drinks beer, existing on a constant diet of Coca-Cola.

Although Jeff is now forty-four years old, his

mother treats him like a little boy. And there is always Greg's ghost in the background of everything they do.

"He was my life," declared Greg in early 1998, as he tried to explain the twins' twisted relationship, by an open fireplace in his mother's front room. "He was me. The only reason we fought was that I wasn't *him*. He would get angry at my weaknesses. He wanted me to be more like him."

Mother and son live together locked in an unspoken guilt about Greg's death, which is always referred to as "an accident."

Ma admits that she doesn't know what really happened between the twins that fateful night, and probably never will.

"Jeff has never had the courage to tell me," she says, adding that she has never asked him.

"I just know that he's my son and I love him. I lost one son. I wasn't going to lose another. I'm a survivor [and] you do what you have to do to get by."

T w o

THE HOUSE OF HORROR

"If I have freedom in my love, And in my soul
am free, Angels alone that soar above,
Enjoy such liberty"
—Richard Lovelace

To all appearances the Hopkins twins had the world on a string. The daughters of a rich, socially prominent Southern family, both were generously gifted with rare beauty and intelligence.

Jane and Jean Hopkins seemed to sail through their youth with effortless ease and could do little wrong. After graduating from their high school with honors, Jean worked for the renowned brokerage house of Goldman Sachs while her Harvard-educated twin sister Jane became a nationally recognized chemical engineer.

As both married and had children they settled down next door to each other in an exclusive Dallas suburb. Living the good life, they mixed in Dallas society and were well respected as pillars of the community.

But there was a terrible curse on the Hopkins sisters, who both secretly battled mental illness. And it would culminate in bloody murder as

Jane and Jean Hopkins made criminal history, becoming the first twins to attempt to kill themselves and their children.

Jane and Jean Hopkins stood out from the rest of the world from the very beginning. Born as leap-year babies on February 29th, 1956, in Van Buren, Arkansas, the twins were the youngest of four children. Their wealthy father Glen Hopkins, Sr., ran a successful furniture store, owned extensive real-estate holdings and was part-owner of a lucrative nursing home.

To the outside world the pretty, dark-haired twins had an idyllic childhood, growing up in the scenic small town on the banks of the Arkansas River. They lived in the lap of luxury in the Hopkins family ancestral home on the town's exclusive Skyline Drive, complete with a swimming pool, gazebo and picnic area. Built on a bluff with panoramic views of the Arkansas River, the two-story home was a well-known Van Buren landmark.

Every summer the family vacationed in Europe, New York and Oklahoma, where they had a holiday home by a lake.

''We led a normal, happy American life,'' remembered their elder brother, Glen Hopkins, Jr., who still runs the family businesses in Van Buren. ''We had a strong family and community upbringing.''

But there was a darker side to the Hopkins family which would come to light many years later when the twins entered therapy. As adults Jane and Jean would both allege that their father had sexually abused them as young children. And the illicit affair of their mother, Ann Hopkins, which resulted in an illegitimate birth, would also prove traumatic for the sisters.

This dysfunctional side of the Hopkins family stayed well-hidden inside the four walls of the family mansion as the twins grew up. To the outside world they were perfectly brought-up young ladies and were embraced by the town as exemplary role models.

But everything changed after their father died suddenly from a heart attack when the twins were twelve years old. Ann Hopkins stepped into the breach, going from full-time housewife to running the family nursing home. Her son Glen Junior, then nineteen, also returned home from college, without a degree, to run the furniture store.

As students at Van Buren High School the Hopkins twins overshadowed their fellow students with brains and beauty. They arrived every morning in identical matching outfits, with their dark wavy hair cut in the same fashionable bob.

Their school friends would remember them as modest, good students who never flaunted their wealth and social advantages to less-fortunate friends.

As the more outgoing twin, Jean made her mark as the queen of Van Buren High School's annual Military Ball and Homecoming Maid of Honor. In her senior year she became student council president.

Jane was quieter and more reserved but also distinguished herself during high school. She served on the student council, and was secretary of the honor society and editor of the student newspaper.

"The twins had it all," says Van Buren's mayor of twenty-five years and the Hopkinses' neighbor, Allen Ray Toothaker. "These were very special young ladies, destined to reach the pinnacle of life. They were brilliant, beautiful, popular."

In 1974 the twins graduated from Van Buren High School with honors and were accepted by the University of Arkansas in Fayetteville, a hundred miles northwest of Van Buren.

The twins easily fell into campus life. They shared the same friends and joined the same sorority, Chi Omega, of which Jane eventually became president. They also served on the same scholastic honor society and Jane pursued her passion for journalism, becoming editor of the university yearbook.

Their classmates recall Jane being the quieter and more conservative of the twins but highly approachable. She preferred to stay in her room and read books and write articles while Jean attended the many campus parties.

Jane was well-respected at the university for her natural political skills, which she needed as editor of the yearbook. She readily mixed with all types of students, from the ultra-conservative classical scholars to the left-wing journalism majors, often calming down her writers during heated yearbook editorial meetings.

In 1978, at the age of twenty-two, the twins graduated with honors from the University of Arkansas and seemed to have the world at their feet. Jane left Fayetteville with a chemical engineering degree, working briefly for IBM before enrolling in Harvard University's business school for a masters in business administration.

Jean also devoted herself to breaking into the business world, enrolling in Southern Methodist University's graduate business school and soon landed a prestigious job at the leading brokerage house of Goldman, Sachs.

"Anything you needed to know about a company, she knew," remembered her Southern Methodist University classmate and friend, Jill McClung.

But unfortunately Jean's personal life was not so successful. After a short-lived marriage in the early 1980s, which ended when she suspected that her husband was gay, she moved to Dallas, Texas, determined to make her mark in society.

She became a member of the Slipper Club, a highly prestigious organization for women, enthusiastically throwing herself into the club's affairs. Before long she was voted club president.

A former Slipper Club member said it was "unfathomable" for someone who wasn't born and raised in Dallas to become accepted, let alone president, of such a snobbish organization.

"It was amazing," the friend said. "It wasn't done."

In 1985, Jean fell in love and married a successful Dallas businessman named Raymond Byrd and seemed to have achieved her long-cherished dream of having a family when, in 1991, she gave birth to a son, Jimmy, followed a year later by another boy, named Riley.

Her twin sister Jane also seemed to be riding on the crest of a wave. After receiving a graduate degree in business, the beautiful twenty-three-year-old married a fellow Harvard student named Clayton C. Elliott, Jr. It was a society wedding that was written up in *The New York Times*.

In early 1986, the newlyweds moved to Houston where Clayton had landed a job with the Hines international real estate company. The next year Jane gave birth to a boy named Clayton Clee Elliott III, followed four years later by a daughter, named Olivia Covington Elliott.

But as the twins' lives publicly blossomed, long-repressed memories of childhood incest began to surface and slowly eat away at their sanity like a cancer.

Soon after her marriage Jean Hopkins-Byrd's well-ordered life began spiraling out of control. She started suffering from depression and entered therapy to try to work things out. Additionally, she was having problems at Goldman Sachs, which ended with her leaving in 1987, amidst bitter personal accusations.

At the same time her sister Jane, who had recently moved next door to Jean in the exclusive Pagewood Drive district of Dallas, was having difficulties in her marriage. In December 1992, Jane and Clayton surprised friends by getting a divorce, citing irreconcilable differences. Clayton went to court for custody of their two children, Clee, five, and one-year-old Olivia, claiming that he was disturbed by Jane's hostility toward them.

Jane was now being treated by the same psychiatrist as her twin sister, and her fragile state of mind was revealed in court papers filed during the custody battle.

"Jane has demonstrated that she can take her anger out against me on the children," her husband testified in court papers. "From a mental health and emotional perspective, Jane has numerous issues she is trying to work through. She is relating to the children the same way she related to me, which was one of the issues that led to our divorce."

In one family evaluation session with Dr. Harold J. Brendel, little Clee suddenly became angry, exclaiming, "I could spit in Mom's face."

And on another occasion with Dr. Brendel, Clee said, "I hope she is not home, don't you, Dad?"

Despite the evidence the court awarded Jane custody of the children and she settled down to her new life as a single mother.

But storm clouds were gathering over both twins as they secretly battled the demons from their past. In June 1994, Jean Hopkins-Byrd was admitted to Zale-Lipshy Hospital after becoming suicidal. She was diagnosed as suffering from psychotic paranoia and doctors treated her mental condition with the anti-psychotic drug Stelazine. Jean responded so well to treatment that she was soon discharged and additionally prescribed two strong anti-depressant drugs, Norpramin and Lorazepam.

Everything was fine until Jean became pregnant in late September, resulting in her doctor taking her off all medicines as a precautionary measure. But she was not warned about possible side-effects of coming off the drugs. Within a few weeks she had a relapse.

Jean started suffering from terrifying delusions and nightmares. She believed that she and her infant sons, Jimmy, three, and Riley, two, were facing torture and certain death from enemies out of her past. And in her deranged state of mind, she decided that the only way to avoid disaster was to kill herself and her children.

One night, in what she tragically viewed as an act of kindness, she gave Jimmy and Riley large doses of the anti-depressant drug Desipramime with their dinner, taking an overdose herself.

Miraculously, Jean and her children were found unconscious and help was summoned in time to save them. Her twin sister Jane watched them being taken away by ambulance to a hospital where they were successfully revived.

Jean Hopkins-Byrd was charged with the attempted murder of her children. A psychiatric report filed with the court revealed her tormented state of mind on the night of the poisonings: ''[Jean] attempted to kill her children and herself,'' it read, ''in the gentlest way she could think of in order to avert the horrors of prolonged suffering, tortures and ultimate death.''

Before her trial Jean was treated at the Timberlawn Psychiatric Hospital in Dallas where she was diagnosed with bipolar mental disorder and given electric shock treatment, Prozac and lithium.

During her sister's slow recovery, Jane helped her young nephews get over their ordeal. She regularly cooked meals for the boys and helped to take care of them.

In June 1996, Jean was found not guilty by reason of insanity. A few months earlier doctors had decided she was back to normal and discharged her from Timberlawn. As she returned home to continue raising her family, her friends noticed a marked change in her behavior. They even felt safe enough to allow her to care for their own children.

"Once they put her on medication, she was like a new person," said family friend and mother of five, Carol Wood.

But a few doors away on Pagewood Drive, Jean's twin sister Jane was struggling to hold on to her own sanity. The murder attempt had been a total shock for Jane, who blamed psychiatry for Jean's actions and stopped her own therapy, telling friends that she no longer approved of it.

"Jane had a general mistrust of the psychiatric field," her ex-husband would later explain.

To outside appearances Jane, now thirty, was the perfect mother. As a newly divorced single mom, she lovingly fussed over Clee, now six, and his two-year-old sister, Olivia, and seemed to think the world of them.

Jane loved reading her favorite Shakespeare and Charles Dickens passages to little Clee and took the children on frequent trips to the zoo and museums to try to broaden their horizons. She joined three library clubs and enthusiastically discussed classic and modern literature, impressing the other members with her keen mind and extensive knowledge.

"You'd see her coming out of the library with thirty books to read to Clee when he was just eighteen months old," said Jane's old college friend Jill McClung.

Every Christmas, Jane would send a New Year greeting card to her friends and family with a collage of pictures of herself and her beautiful children. On the surface they seemed like the all-American family. Some even compared her to Jackie Kennedy, for her vivacious looks and apparent mothering skills.

Friends would later recall Jane's utter distaste for the media's depiction of violence against children. She had been most upset when one of her literary groups discussed author Toni Morrison's book *Beloved*, where the leading character kills her own child.

"She didn't like to hear stories where kids were hurt or killed," said family friend Tom Keener. "I always attributed it to her being upset over what happened with her sister. [But] maybe she had a fear of her own capabilities in this area."

In December 1996, Jane moved the children across Dallas to University Park so that Clee and Olivia could have more children to play with. Her sister Jean's family had recently moved to Plano and Jane said that she too needed a change of scene.

Her children were delighted by their new

$300,000 two-story luxury home on Purdue Street, and adapted easily. They loved their new surroundings and would ride their bicycles up and down the street while Jane sat reading on the patio.

Olivia was an angelic-looking five-year-old who had inherited her mother's love of learning. Bright and spunky, she loved swimming, bicycling and playing with her stuffed animals.

Clee was in third grade at the Oak Hill Academy and was a good student. The cheerful, handsome nine-year-old passionately loved baseball, playing catcher for his school team, and could talk for hours about batting averages. Jane proudly boasted to friends about his academic progress and had arranged for him to move to the nearer Robert S. Hyer Elementary School the following school year, where he would be joined by Olivia when she started kindergarten.

To their new neighbors in University Park, the Hopkinses seemed a normal, happy family and the perfect addition to the upscale community. But behind closed doors things were very different.

Soon after the move, Jane Hopkins began displaying the exact same disturbing signs of mental instability that her twin sister had two years earlier. In a macabre déjà vu she began telling friends that a figure from her past was stalking her and the children and wanted to harm them. She said that her house was under constant surveillance, and regularly checked under her car to ensure that a bomb hadn't been planted there.

Jane was constantly in motion, finding it hard to sit still and focus on anything. She became obsessed with her physical health, believing that she had lupus, a disease of the immune system that strikes many young women. When doctors pronounced her healthy she refused to believe them.

Over the next few months Jane began to withdraw from the world and distance herself from her family. And like her twin before her, she began telling friends that she had been sexually abused as a young child.

As Jane Hopkins slipped deeper and deeper into madness, her frustrated family and friends were powerless to stop her.

"I knew Jane was depressed," said her friend Tom Keener. "I couldn't take a gun to her head and make her get help."

Over the final few months, as her mind became increasingly tortured, Jane struggled to maintain a degree of normality for the outside world. When she occasionally let her guard slip and confided her delusions, no one ever dreamed that family history might repeat itself— this time with tragic results.

Every night she could see the enemy driving up and down the street, watching; always watching. They'd park on the street opposite her house and spy. She'd even seen them peering through the living room window.

She knew that her pursuers were real and would stop at nothing. They were closing in for the kill. But no one understood when she told them. Her friends and family all thought she was crazy.

Jane Hopkins made up her mind over the weekend. It had been a hard decision but it was the only way out. They could attack at any time. As a mother she feared far more for Clee and Olivia than for herself. But she realized that out of kindness, she would have to be brave. The alternatives were unthinkable.

Although she loved the children more than life itself, she now knew there was only one escape from the evil forces that pursued her.

On Monday, July 28, 1997, Clayton Elliott was scheduled to return with Clee and Olivia from a four-day vacation to Disney World in Orlando. Jane Hopkins had spent the weekend at home alone, telephoning friends and family, and seemed to have lost all touch with reality.

After hearing Jane's ravings her family began to fear for Clee and Olivia's safety. They decided to intervene and advise Clayton to take them away as quickly as possible.

"She was totally out of control," said her brother-in-law Raymond Byrd, who was well aware of how his wife had tried to kill their children. "She was absolutely paranoid in the last few days. We came to the conclusion that she should not be alone with her children.''

That Monday, Jane's concerned elder sister, Linda Morgan, who had received several disturbing telephone calls from Jane to her home in Albuquerque, New Mexico, left an urgent message for Clayton to call Raymond Byrd on his return from Disney World. But Clayton didn't get the message until Tuesday afternoon—a few hours after he had returned the children to Jane.

Finally reaching Clayton by telephone, Byrd warned him that his ex-wife needed immediate help and his children were at risk. Byrd briefed him on the situation, saying that he had spoken to his sister-in-law that day and begged her to seek help. Jane had grudgingly agreed to do so, he said, but feared that a counselor would report her to the police, who might take away the children.

That night Clayton drove to University Park and persuaded Jane to let him take Clee and Olivia home with him. He assured her that it was only a temporary arrangement and she could have them back at any time.

When Jane arrived at his house at 9:30 a.m. the next morning she seemed rational and happier than he'd seen her in a long time. She promised to get counseling and her positive outlook reassured him that everything would be fine. He felt safe giving her back the children, relieved that she had come to her senses. He kissed his children good-bye and they walked down the driveway and got into Jane's car.

It would be the last time he would ever see his family alive again.

After arriving back in University Park, Jane gathered her treasured family photo albums and wrapped them up in gift paper. She told the children to be good and play and she would be back in a few minutes.

Driving to a nearby friend's house, Jane handed over the photo albums with instructions to give them to her ex-husband. Then, without a further word of explanation, she rushed back to her car and drove home.

Jane had spent the previous night preparing for death. As she sat in the armchair in her living room listening to her favorite pieces of classical music, Jane felt a strange peace come over her as she carefully wrote six suicide notes in black felt-tip pen. They would explain everything.

It was nearly midday as Jane began attaching the notes to walls all over the house. As she stuck the last note to the medicine cabinet door in the bathroom, she began to cry.

"THEY ARE ANGELS," it read. "PRAY FOR US. FORGIVE ME."

Then Jane composed herself and walked toward the kitchen. She took a six-inch serrated carving knife from a drawer and went upstairs to where Clee was reading a fairy-tale book to Olivia. Her eyes blazed as she walked into the bedroom with the knife hidden behind her.

"Can you come downstairs for a second, honey?" she called gently. The little boy gave the book to his sister and obediently followed his mother downstairs. As he walked into the kitchen Jane rushed toward him with a look in her eyes that he'd never seen before. The boy screamed as he saw the flash of the long steel knife she was holding.

"No, Mom! No, Mom!" he shouted as his mother began stabbing him.

Clee screamed in pain as she plunged the knife into his chest and the blood spurted. He began running away as his young sister, paralyzed in fear upstairs, started to cry. Jane chased him out of the kitchen and into the backyard as he desperately pleaded with her to stop.

Finally, his mother cornered him against the garden wall and began thrusting the long knife into his throat and chest. She kept plunging it in again and again until his anguished cries turned to whimpers, finally stopping altogether. The tears rolled down her face as she dragged her son's blood-soaked body back into the kitchen and left him on the floor.

After closing the door to the kitchen, Jane returned upstairs to complete her mission. She found Olivia cowering in fear in her bedroom. As if in a trance, Jane tried to soothe her little daughter as she forced her into the bathroom.

Once inside she wrenched off the sliding shower door, wedged it against the bathroom door barricading them in, and turned on the shower.

She barely heard her daughter's screams as she began the butchery, thrusting the knife into her daughter repeatedly until Olivia lay motionless on the white tile floor, her blood being washed away by the shower water.

In a moment of clarity, Jane stopped and said a prayer for her children. She thanked God that they were finally safe and that He had given her the strength to free them from this cruel world forever. Soon they would all be in heaven together.

Then she raised the knife above her head and, using all her strength, plunged it straight into her heart and kept stabbing until everything went black.

At eight o'clock that night Clayton Elliott arrived at the house to tell his ex-wife that he had spoken to a psychiatrist and arranged counseling for her. He unlocked the front door and walked into the kitchen, where he found his son's body lying on the floor in a pool of blood.

He began screaming in shock and staggered into the hallway to dial 911.

"My son has been murdered!" he hysterically told dispatcher Cathy Marr. "My son has been murdered! My ex-wife and daughter are missing."

He rushed out of the house to next-door neighbor Carolyn Columbo, and tearfully told her that Clee had been murdered and his body was stone cold.

"I can't find [Jane] anywhere," he wailed. "I don't know where she is and my son's dead!"

By the time the police arrived a few minutes later, scores of neighbors, some still wearing bedroom clothes and slippers, were lining the street to see what was going on. Detectives entered the house to discover Clee lying dead in the kitchen. They went upstairs, forced open the barricaded bathroom, and recoiled in horror, seeing the bodies of Jane Hopkins and her daughter Olivia lying in the shower. The water was still running over the bodies, which had stained the white tiles red.

As they cordoned off the house as a crime scene, a blonde woman suddenly drove up. She had a few words with Clayton and then had to be restrained by police as she tried to run into the house.

"She murdered him!" the woman started screaming to Elliot. "I told you she would do something like that!" Then she jumped into her car and drove off.

Over the next few days, Jane Hopkins' family and friends tried to make sense of the carnage. Although there had been warning signs that something was wrong, they could not believe that Jane could possibly have slaughtered her own children in such brutal fashion.

"The act is totally, completely insane," declared her brother-in-law Raymond Byrd, refusing to discuss any connection to his own wife's murder attempt. "I know that [Jane] has had psychological counseling. I don't know what her issues were. I can't begin to get inside her mind and know what she is feeling."

The day after the murders the Dallas County medical examiner's office ruled Clee's and Olivia's deaths as homicides and Jane's as suicide. Each had died of multiple stab wounds.

"We don't have a murderer running loose," declared University Park Police Chief Bob Dixon. "From the way the notes read, it caused us to believe it was a suicide-murder. It's just tragic."

As Jane's body was taken back to her home town of Van Buren to be buried in the Hopkins family plot, many questioned if a genetic defect could account for the twins' violence against their children.

University of Richmond neuroscientist Dr. Craig Kinsley said the fact that Jean had also tried to kill her children offered vital clues.

"There's a possibility that there's a genetic influence on a display of such . . . behavior," he said. "It suggests there could be a biological reason why these two women would display indifferent or abusive behavior to their children."

On the Monday after the killings, Clee and Olivia were buried at the Highland Park Presbyterian Church in an hour-long service, billed as a celebration of their lives. The little church was packed with mourners who solemnly filed by the children's identical ivory-and-gold–trimmed coffins, covered in flowers.

The Reverend Joseph Parker summed up the feelings of the shocked community, saying, "[It's] a tragedy which literally knocks us to our knees."

One of Clayton Junior's teachers, Debbie Hall, read aloud to the mourners, among whom were many of the children's friends, a moving tribute she'd written.

"Clee's no longer with us, through no fault of his own," it read. "Clee's no longer with us, for his little soul has gone home."

Two weeks later Clayton Elliott, Jr., broke his silence to announce that he had set up a foundation in his son and daughter's memories to raise money for children's charities.

"I am still struggling with why this happened," said Elliott. "Naturally, you wonder what I could have done differently to have almost any other outcome. Unfortunately, we will not know that answer in this world."

Twenty miles north, in Plano, Jean Hopkins-Byrd refused to discuss the murders. She will be under medication for the rest of her life. Raymond Byrd says he has no new fears for their children, and that Jean now leads a happy and productive life as a wife and mother and is fully cured.

In 1997 the Byrds filed a civil suit in Dallas County against psychiatrist Dr. Leonora Stephens, accusing her of failing to properly diagnose and evaluate Jean's condition before her suicide and murder attempts in 1994.

As of going to press, the matter remains unresolved.

Three

GOOD TWIN/EVIL TWIN

"We are spinning our own fates, good or evil,
and never to be undone"
—The Principles of Psychology, ch. 4

Were Sunny and Gina Han the definitive "good and evil twins" as they would be branded by Los Angeles detectives in a bizarre morality tale that gripped America? Or was it the ultimate case of sibling rivalry gone mad, with Gina plotting to murder Sunny and assume her identity to erase her own criminal past?

Once the strikingly beautiful twenty-three-year-old South Korean–born identical twins had been the best of friends. But jealousy and greed had finally torn them apart as they grew up seeking the American dream.

While Sunny graduated from high school with honors and entered college, Gina struggled to make ends meet as a casino croupier. Becoming addicted to gambling, she robbed family and friends to pay off her mounting debts.

The twins became mortal enemies after Sunny caught her sister stealing and called the police. When Gina was sent to jail for six

months she blamed Sunny, hatching a convo-
luted murder plot to get revenge.

Although Sunny was just five minutes older
than her twin sister Gina, the consequences
would be immeasurable. For under the
traditions of South Korean culture, Sunny, as
the first-born, was the privileged child, receiving far more respect than Gina, who was expected to defer to her.

From their earliest days Gina and Sunny
were impossible to tell apart. As chubby-faced
toddlers, their parents dressed them alike in expensive baby clothes imported from America.
Growing up in poverty-stricken South Korea,
they enjoyed an affluent childhood as the pam-
pered daughters of a successful middle-class
engineer, Yun Heo, and his wife Boo.

When they were twelve their lives changed
forever when their parents divorced. The family
broke up and Boo emigrated to America with
her twin daughters, while their father stayed behind in South Korea. It was a traumatic time
for the girls as Gina sided with the father she
adored and Sunny supported their mother.

The Hans settled in Anaheim, Southern California, and faced an uphill struggle as faceless
Korean immigrants, not speaking a word of English. In order to survive, their attractive mother
took a job as a bar hostess to support the family.
She would often neglect her twin daughters,

disappearing for days at a time to gamble with her many boyfriends.

The teenage sisters, who were now enrolled in the local high school, were often left alone without food or supervision, feeling unloved and unwanted. It was a highly traumatic time for the twins, who believed they had been abandoned in a strange land and were on their own.

"[Mom] was more of an abuser than a discipliner," Gina Han would later tell a psychiatrist.

Their lives improved when they turned sixteen in 1991, and were sent to live with their Aunt Sonya and her husband, James Norris. When the girls arrived at the small town of Pine Valley, fifty miles east of San Diego, they hardly spoke English, even though they had been in America four years.

The Norrises enrolled them at Mount Empire High School in the middle of their junior year. It wasn't long before the twins proved themselves highly intelligent and academically gifted.

The twins quickly mastered English, easily overtaking their classmates to get to the top of the class. They were seen as serious and dedicated students by their teachers, who admired their relentless drive and ambition.

Gina and Sunny were popular with the other students but preferred spending their free time with each other, studying pocket English dictionaries to enlarge their vocabularies.

The slender young twins looked so alike that their classmates couldn't tell them apart, constantly mixing them up. So in order to differentiate themselves, Gina cut her long silky black hair into bangs while Sunny kept hers long.

But although they were physically alike, Sunny and Gina had diametrically opposite personalities. Sunny was a happy, fun-loving extrovert with a great sense of humor, making her the class favorite. Gina was quieter and more serious, often appearing jealous of her sister's new-found popularity.

When Sunny started dating the young son of a neighbor, the Norrises did not approve. So she moved in with the boy's family across the street, leaving Gina alone with her adoptive family.

During their final school years, the Han twins strove even harder to succeed and were inconsolable if they got anything less than ''A'' grades in every subject. Yet while they constantly competed in their studies and relationships, they would always help each other and were best friends and allies.

But when they graduated as co-valedictorians in their eighty-student class in 1993, their lives veered off in different directions as they started making their own ways in the world.

After high school, Sunny enrolled at the University of LaVerne outside Los Angeles while

Gina joined the Air Force, quitting after only a few weeks. Every week Sunny received a check for $1,000 from her family, which she put in a joint-access account to share with her twin. But Gina, who was now living in the San Diego suburb of El Cajon, complained to her roommates that she wasn't receiving her fair share and swore to get even. She became increasingly jealous of Sunny's affluent new student lifestyle, which included driving an expensive BMW and always wearing expensive clothes and make-up.

Exactly how Sunny Han paid for her expensive tastes mystified friends, who speculated that she secretly moonlighted as an exotic dancer. Years later she would deny using her perfect body to finance her high-living lifestyle, declaring, ''I am not a topless dancer at a bar, I'm not a prostitute, and I'm not a drug dealer.''

In 1993 Sunny was arrested for stealing a friend's credit card and going on a $1,300 shopping spree, buying designer jeans, lingerie, shoes and sunglasses. She blithely told police that her victim wouldn't mind as she came from a ''very rich'' family. In court Sunny admitted illegal credit-card use and was fined $405 and placed on three years' probation.

In an attempt to keep up with her sister, Gina found a well-paid job as a blackjack dealer at the Barona Casino on an Indian reservation in Lakeside, California, but she too broke the law after running up huge gambling losses at high-stakes blackjack.

To finance her escalating gambling habit Gina began forging checks for up to $40,000, even robbing her former guardian and uncle, James Norris.

In May 1996 the sisters moved in together at an apartment in Placentia, California, and constantly fought. Police had to be called on four occasions to stop fist fights between the twins. On one occasion Sunny punched her sister in the face, breaking her nose.

Things came to a head when Gina stole Sunny's car and credit cards and went on a spending spree for designer clothes.

"She wanted that BMW," said Diane Caradine, one of Gina's friends. "And she didn't care how she got it."

Sunny called the police and Gina was arrested for burglary and grand theft, and was sentenced to six months in jail. After serving three months behind bars she was transferred to a work furlough program, so she could hold down a job during the day. But every night and on weekends she had to return to jail.

That spring, relations between the twins seemed to have improved. Sunny regularly visited her sister in jail and called her five times a week. But they soured again after Sunny refused to allow Gina to move into her luxurious new Irvine condominium when she finished her sentence.

Gina was furious, breaking off all contact with her sister. She then decided to get even with Sunny and kill her so that she could assume her twin's identity and make a fresh start.

On October 27, 1996, Gina left jail on a work furlough pass and went on the run. With a warrant out for her arrest she fled to El Cajon, California, where she got an apartment and began to search for a hit man to murder Sunny, surprising friends by asking, "Who wants to help me kill my sister?"

A week later, Gina drove down to Sunny's condo in Irvine with two friends, nineteen-year-old Robyn Weatherby, and Arkisha Moore, eighteen, to pick up some property and a car that belonged to her. During the ninety-mile drive north on Interstate 5, Gina startled the girls by asking if they knew anyone who would kill her twin sister.

"I want this bitch dead," she declared, offering the girls $100 to "beat the crap out of her."

When the girls asked why she wanted to murder her own sister, Gina said that Sunny would kill her first if she didn't. She explained that Sunny had beaten her up in the past and had a boyfriend in an Asian gang. The two girls thought Gina was joking.

But they began to take her more seriously when they arrived at Sunny's apartment on Jefferson Street in Irvine. Gina knocked at the door and when there was no answer she walked back to the car, announcing that she would wait for Sunny to return and then kill her. While they waited outside in the car, Gina showed them plastic bags she had brought to clean up any mess afterward. The girls were so horrified they made Gina drive them home immediately.

The following day, Gina finally recruited two teenage hit men to murder Sunny. She hired Arkisha Moore's seventeen-year-old cousin, Archie Bryant, and his friend John Sayarath, sixteen, who both agreed to do the job for $100 each.

Gina hired a rental car from Avis and during the ninety-minute drive north to Irvine showed the boys a gun, saying that she wanted to kill her sister herself. The boys' job would be to bind and gag Sunny and then call Gina to finish her off.

At lunchtime they stopped at Ralphs supermarket in Irvine to purchase supplies for the murder. Gina bought twine and duct tape to tie up Sunny and two pairs of gloves, plastic bags and Lysol to clean up any evidence.

Then they lunched at a Carl's Jr. restaurant where Gina gave the boys a final briefing on what to do and the directions to Sunny's home.

At about 1 p.m. the trio drew up outside Sunny's apartment. Sayarath knocked on the door, which was answered by Sunny's roommate, Angie Woo, who said that everyone was out. When the nervous teenager tried to talk his way inside, posing as a magazine salesman, she closed the door on him.

An hour later he made a second attempt but Woo still refused to let him in. Gina then tried a new ploy and told the super that she had lost her key, but he refused to help.

An angry Gina went back to the car, ordering her "hit men" to get into the apartment and not come back until they had tied Sunny up and she was ready to be executed.

By this time Sunny Han had returned home and was dressing while her roommate, Helen Kim, played Nintendo. When the doorbell rang, Kim answered to find Bryant on the doorstep selling magazines. After scanning the magazines, Kim told Bryant that she wasn't interested and was about to close the door when Sayarath appeared from nowhere. The men forced their way into the apartment with guns drawn, ordering Kim to the floor.

"Please don't hurt me!" screamed Kim as Sayarath duct-taped her mouth and tied her hands behind her back, while Bryant went off in search of Sunny Han.

Hearing the screams, Sunny thought Kim was being raped and locked herself in the bathroom with her cellular phone. She dialed 911 and reported that burglars were raping her friend.

Suddenly, in the middle of the call, Bryant burst in and threw her to the floor. Aiming his loaded gun at her head, he demanded to know if she had called the police. Keeping cool, Sunny managed to turn off the phone, telling him she had only been speaking to a friend.

Then Bryant forced Sunny into the bedroom and threatened to shoot her as he gagged her with duct tape and bound her hands behind her back.

While Sunny was being tied up, Helen Kim managed to free herself and made a run for it. But before she could reach the front door, Bryant intercepted her and forced her back, saying, "I should shoot you for trying that."

The teenage hit men then carried the girls, bound and gagged, into the bathroom and threw them into the tub. As they lay facing each other and waiting to die, they heard their attackers in Sunny's bedroom, going through her things.

"Go and get Gina from the car so she can finish off her sister," Sunny heard Bryant say to Sayarath, as the horrific realization hit her that her twin sister was somehow involved in the attack.

Suddenly police sirens could be heard in the distance as officers responded to Sunny's 911 call. Bryant immediately rushed into the bathroom and began swearing as he ripped the duct tape off the girls' faces and untied them.

"Tell the cops it's a joke," he shouted as he freed them.

When police arrived at the apartment complex, they found Gina coolly sitting in the car with Sayarath. After calmly identifying herself to police, Gina said that she lived in the apartment and had just had a fight with one of her roommates.

"Is there anything wrong?" she kept asking the officer innocently.

Then Bryant dashed out of the apartment and, as soon as he saw police, ran back inside. A few minutes later he reappeared with Sunny and Helen Kim and gave himself up. While he was being arrested, Gina and Sayarath drove off, abandoning Bryant to his fate.

Now on the run, Gina headed south to San Diego, attempting to use one of Sunny's credit cards to lease a Nissan car in San Juan Capistrano. But the salesman was suspicious, telling her to come back in twenty-four hours so he could check her credit history. Then she drove to a Wells Fargo bank and, pretending to be Sunny, withdrew $5,000 from her sister's account so they could flee the country.

But police were hot on their trail and had issued an all points bulletin throughout Southern California with their descriptions. A few hours later Gina and Sayarath were arrested at police gunpoint when they dropped off their hired car at the Alamo Car Rental at San Diego Airport.

Gina was brought into custody and held for conspiracy to commit murder and four other felonies. Soon after, she telephoned her shocked twin sister to explain herself.

"I wish you were dead," a tearful Sunny told her during an emotional conversation.

The day after her arrest Gina—who now faced twenty-six years to life in prison—described the twins' telephone call to reporters from her cell in Orange County Jail.

"She was really mad," Gina told a reporter. "She told me I need psychiatric help [and that] I should go to prison for twenty years—she's having a kick out of my being in jail."

The astonishing story of Gina's "murder for hire" scheme to kill her twin made headlines around the world.

"It's almost like a movie plot," explained Irvine Police Sergeant Al Murray. "She evidently had been conspiring for some time."

Over the next few weeks, Sunny Han became a national celebrity as tabloid TV and talk shows offered big money for her story. She came out of hiding to receive $15,000 to appear on *Hard Copy* and was interviewed by Geraldo Riviera for a show entitled *Twin Horrors: The Horrible Things Twins Can Do to Each Other*. Sunny was also reportedly offered up to $2 million for the movie rights to her story.

But friends and family still found it hard to believe that the gifted twin sisters—who had seemed like poster children for the immigrant success story in America—could have become such murderous enemies.

"These are top-of-the-line girls," explained their cousin, Jim Norris. "They were valedictorians and were always close. I don't know what to say.''

On November 22, Gina Han appeared in Harbor Municipal Court in Newport Beach and was officially charged with conspiracy to commit murder, robbery, assault, burglary, false imprisonment and criminal conspiracy. She was ordered to return to jail without bail until her arraignment.

Three months later Sunny visited Gina in jail for the first time since the arrest. In an emotional reunion Gina protested her innocence, eventually persuading her twin that she had merely been a pawn in an elaborate scam by the two other teenagers.

''We were all crying today,'' Sunny said as she left the jail with her mother Boo. ''She's not been plotting this. I'm one hundred percent sure. There's no way she could have done this.''

Their jailhouse meeting convinced Sunny that Gina was completely innocent and she now claimed that police had brainwashed her into thinking that her sister wanted her dead.

''I thought it was totally absurd,'' she said. ''But I started to believe the police. I was confused. I thought maybe it was possible.''

From then on Sunny would become her twin sister's biggest supporter and advocate, even making an emotionally charged appearance on the ''Leeza Show'' to campaign on Gina's behalf.

On March 11, 1997, the Han twins—now twenty-two—met again in court for a day-long preliminary hearing. Gina entered the courtroom first, wearing shackles and a blue jail jumpsuit. She looked depressed and carefully avoided all eye contact.

In stark contrast, Sunny arrived a few minutes later with her newly hired media spokeswoman. Wearing a fashionable dress and heavy make-up, she enthusiastically smiled for the flashing cameras and TV news crews.

After the hearing Sunny Han gave an impromptu press conference outside the court, declaring her twin sister's innocence.

"My sister isn't guilty," she said. "If anyone is jealous it would be me of her. She's smarter and more artistic. Somehow, she got scammed by those two boys."

Deputy Public Defender Roger Alexander, who was defending Gina, said no one should be surprised that Sunny was sticking by her Gina.

"Let's face it," he told reporters. "They want to love each other. They are sisters."

Gina Han's trial began in Santa Ana on October 30, 1997, in a blaze of publicity. Court TV cameras were inside the courtroom to carry gavel-to-gavel coverage to an estimated thirty-two million homes, with producers hoping it would become as addictive as the O. J. Simpson trial. Almost overshadowed in the dock were

Archie Bryant and John Sayarath, who faced the same charges as Gina.

In his opening statements prosecutor Bruce Moore told jurors that Gina had wanted her twin sister dead at least six months before the alleged attempt. But defense lawyers for Sayarath and Bryant maintained that things had spun out of control and rather than being "a recipe for murder" it was "a recipe for disaster."

Throughout the testimony Gina Han, wearing a simple gray-and-black dress, diligently took notes as witness after witness took the stand to testify against her.

On the second day of the trial, Sunny Han had to be smuggled into court through the back door to avoid the hundreds of reporters and TV crews who were anticipating her taking the stand for the prosecution.

The atmosphere was electric as a nervous-looking Sunny, wearing a fashionable periwinkle jumpsuit and spiked heels, crossed the packed courtroom to testify about her sister's alleged attempt to murder her.

Speaking in a shaky whisper, she told how the twins had come to America and that, although they had "hit, scratched and pinched" each other since childhood, they had remained close. "Come on, we're sisters," she explained, smiling at Gina.

Describing her love–hate relationship with Gina, Sunny admitted hitting her sister in the face during an argument over Gina's boyfriend the previous year. But, she said, they loved one another and never wanted to kill each other.

The following day the trial had to be delayed when Sunny was late. As she stumbled into the courtroom more than an hour behind schedule it was obvious that something was wrong. Her pretty face was puffy and she looked dazed and disoriented, almost collapsing three times on the way to the witness stand to continue her testimony. Each time she had to be caught by bailiffs, who helped her back to her feet.

When Sunny finally reached the stand she and Gina were just a few feet apart. They both avoided looking at each other.

In a moment of high drama, Superior Court Judge Eileen C. Moore asked Sunny to explain her lateness. The star witness looked confused and was slurring her words badly. She told the judge that she had just taken a drug overdose after having a fight with her mother and breaking up with her boyfriend.

"I went to the drugstore and bought three boxes of sleeping pills," she whispered in a barely audible voice. "Each box contained twenty pills."

As the judge suggested that she be taken to a room to compose herself, there was a general gasp from spectators as Sunny lost her balance and almost collapsed. Bailiffs rushed to her aid, helping her down from the witness stand and out of the court.

Moments later a bailiff rushed back into the courtroom and picked up the telephone, shouting, "I need paramedics. We have a female adult. She took three boxes of sleeping pills."

While recovering in the intensive care unit of Western General Hospital, Sunny admitted washing down the sleeping pills with a bottle of beer to avoid another day of damaging testimony against her sister.

"I didn't want to go back to court," she explained. "I thought maybe if I don't testify . . . it will be better for my sister."

The following day, as her overdose cast a long shadow over the trial, the defense sought access to Sunny's medical records, asking the judge to declare a mistrial.

After three days in the hospital Sunny was released and returned to court on November 12 to complete her testimony. Looking remarkably fresh and well-groomed after her ordeal, she wept uncontrollably as she told of the twins' unhappy childhood in South Korea and their new life in America.

"We went shopping," she sobbed as Gina too broke down in tears in the defendant's box a few feet away. "We went out drinking to a club. We watched movies all the time. I tell her everything."

But, she said, everything changed in March 1996 when Gina stole money from her. In the following months the twins fought so violently

that police were called on four separate occasions to calm them down.

By the fall of 1997 Sunny had broken off
relations with Gina, refusing to give her her
new phone number and address in Irvine. When
Gina finally tracked her down, Sunny wouldn't
even allow her to come in and collect an IRS
check and a pair of shoes.

Later, when asked by the defense about her
lucrative television appearances and a possible
movie deal, Sunny expressed no qualms about
cashing in on the notoriety of the case.

"If I was to make money, yes I'd like to,"
she said. "Regardless of what my feelings are,
people are interested in it. What can I do about
it?"

Asked if she had taken an overdose to make
herself more marketable, Sunny denied it, saying that she was emotionally depressed about
the case.

"I can't even explain to myself why I did
it," she told the jury.

Despite much speculation that Gina would
take the stand in her own defense, she was ad-
vised by her lawyers not to testify. Throughout
the trial Gina had been convinced that she
would go free and was already making plans
for her future.

A month before the trial she wrote to a recently released fellow prisoner, describing the
new life she was planning in Beverly Hills. In
the handwritten letter, on floral-print stationery,

Gina said that she wanted to study at either the University of California or the University of Southern California and get a job in a clothing store.

"I was really hoping to be out next week," she wrote. "But unfortunately my trial won't be done until the second week of November. Gosh, I can hardly wait."

On November 20, Gina Han was convicted of conspiring to murder her twin sister, in addition to four other felonies, including illegal possession of a firearm. Her two co-defendants, Archie Bryant and John Sayarath, were also found guilty of all charges. They all faced spending the rest of their lives behind bars.

As the verdict was read Gina's lip began quivering uncontrollably as she broke down in tears. Sunny Han, who watched the verdict live on television in her apartment, also wept.

"I'm pretty shocked," she told reporters straight afterward. "I thought it was going to go the other way. When you think about whose fault it was it was probably my fault. It's me."

She then accused the media of distorting the twins' relationship, vowing to stand by her sister.

"There is no such thing as good and evil twins," she explained. "I want people to know that I love her and my sister loves me . . . no matter what others say."

In January 1998 the defense motion for a

new trial was rejected. On May 8, 1998, Gina Han was sentenced to serve twenty-six years to life in jail; Archie Bryant received sixteen years and John Sayarath got eight years and four months, which was put on hold to see if he would benefit by serving his time in the California Youth Authority.

Before sentencing, Gina tearfully begged Judge Eileen Moore for mercy.

"Sunny is my flesh and blood, and she believes in me one hundred percent," she pleaded. "I feel very bad for all the pain I've caused my community and family."

Four

THE BLACK WIDOWS

"This is the Black Widow, death"
—By Robert Traill and Spence Lowell.
Mr. Edwards and the Spider

D r. Jack Wilson looked at his watch and sighed. Although he was already two hours late he was in no hurry to go home to his wife Betty. The genial middle-aged eye surgeon deliberately stalled for time, sitting at his desk preparing patients' reports that could easily have waited. Anything to delay leaving the security of his office for the uncertainties of home.

It was 6 p.m. on the Friday before Memorial Day and he was the last person in the entire building. Everyone else had left early, eager to begin the much-anticipated three-day weekend. But Dr. Wilson was dreading the prospect of his "second honeymoon" trip to Santa Fe with Betty.

It was a last desperate attempt for a reconciliation to save their ailing seventeen-year marriage. Although he'd built up one of the most successful ophthalmic practices in Huntsville, Alabama, from scratch, a ready smile and cornball sense of humor belied his bitter failure as a husband.

The tiny, frail-looking fifty-five-year-old doctor with the walrus mustache and heavy spectacles had once been ridiculed. But over the years he had learned to deliberately play up his eccentricities, endearing him to patients who often left his office in fits of laughter.

He would do anything to get a laugh. His wacky sense of humor included wearing Christmas ties in the summer, and even his prescription pad bore the motto, "Best Eye Doctor in the Known Universe." He often took his shoes off during eye examinations, saying that it made him feel more comfortable padding around in socks in his office, which was full of his treasured Elvis Presley memorabilia.

Long hours and an obsessive drive to succeed had made him a multimillionaire and even something of a celebrity in Huntsville. He was well known for his frequent appearances on television and radio talk shows, where he loved to recount his favorite practical jokes.

Dr. Wilson was also an active political fundraiser in Huntsville, where he and Betty were firmly established on the society "A" list. Only the previous night they had attended a party to launch their friend Tim Morgan's run for the upcoming district attorney elections.

But beneath the public façade of success and affluence Dr. Wilson was a deeply unhappy man. A few years earlier he had had most of his intestine removed and had to wear a colostomy bag. When the strong drugs used to treat the disease had rendered him impotent, Betty Wilson had embarked on numerous affairs with men she met at her Alcoholics Anonymous meetings.

She often boasted about her sexual exploits—many taking place in the Wilsons' marital bed—saying that her husband was most understanding and wanted her to be happy.

The 1992 Memorial Day trip to Santa Fe was Dr. Wilson's final attempt to repair his marriage. And as he peered out of his office window at the falling darkness over Huntsville, he was not optimistic about the outcome.

Betty Wilson had always told her twin sister, Peggy Lowe, everything. Although Peggy lived ninety miles away in Talladega, Alabama, they talked on the telephone several times a day. Theirs had always been a close relationship ever since a miserable childhood, when they'd been forced to rely on each other to survive.

The twins were born on July 14, 1945, in the tiny mill city of East Gadsden, Alabama, lying at the foot of the Appalachian Mountains. Their father, Oscar Woods, was a police officer who ruled the town with an iron hand. A hard-drinking self-proclaimed racist, ''Wormy'' Woods, as he was nicknamed, terrorized the poor black community with his bullying tactics, which often verged on violence.

After going off duty he would bring his drunken aggression into the house, often physically abusing the twins and their two elder sisters, GeDelle and Martha. Little Betty and Peggy dreaded his coming home in a drunken rage. On bad nights he'd shine a flashlight in their eyes to wake them up and then make them eat Ben Gay ointment for his amusement.

"My father was an abusive alcoholic," Peggy would later remember. "When I was in junior high school, I started realizing that we had a very atypical home."

Peggy took care of her sister from the beginning. Far more beautiful and gifted than her fraternal twin, Peggy became Betty's protector. As children the twins locked themselves in the bathroom for hours to create their own fantasy world, far from their father's cruel bullying. It was Peggy who would soothe Betty and teach her to avoid Wormy's violent temper tantrums by hiding when he came home after a day of drinking.

Although often physically abused herself, their mother, Nell, was the single ray of sunlight in the Woodses' house. To supplement her husband's meager wages from the police department, Nell worked long hours doing piecework in a factory, making dry-cleaning hangers.

An extremely house-proud and devoted mother, Nell spent most of her hard-earned wages on the twins, ensuring that they always looked smart and presentable. One Saturday each month she would walk Peggy and Betty into town for lunch and then go shopping to buy them new outfits.

As teenagers the beautiful Peggy Woods seemed to overshadow her plainer twin in every way. "Peggy was the girl next door," said one of her former classmates. "She was cute, popular and sweet."

In 1962 she was crowned the Queen of Gadsden High School at the school's annual coronation ball by a panel of judges that included popular TV-show host Art Linkletter.

Reputed to be the most beautiful girl in town, Peggy's teenage years were strewn with trophies and accolades. Although she came from the wrong side of town, the popular beauty found all social doors open to her. She was constantly asked out on dates by Huntsville's most eligible young men, unlike her plainer twin sister.

The shyer Betty paled into insignificance next to her golden twin. Although she strove to find her own place in the sun, Betty always seemed to be following in Peggy's footsteps. She had to make do with joining the high school drama group and although the twins were inseparable, many of their friends believed that Betty was jealous, deeply resenting her sister's success.

While Peggy seemed to lead a charmed life, getting good grades and never getting into trouble, Betty became a bad girl, developing a strong rebellious streak. She stayed out late drinking with boys, and often skipped school in open defiance of her teachers and parents.

But in her late teens Betty suddenly came into her own, discovering a new confidence that surprised many. Almost overnight she began to dominate Peggy, who was far less ambitious and materialistic.

The twins' lives appeared to be heading down the same track after they graduated from high school, deciding not to go to college. Both married in 1964 and had babies almost immediately. But within four years the twins had divorced and were back on their own.

While Peggy remained in East Gadsden and married the local choir director, Wayne Lowe, Betty headed for the bright lights of Huntsville, looking for freedom and excitement.

In the early 1970s the picturesque northern Alabama city was a magnet for many ambitious young people like Betty who were seeking the good life. Nestled on the flatland in the shadow of Garth Mountain, Huntsville owed its prosperity to the Marshall Space Flight Center and scores of high-technology companies which provided jobs and security.

Leaving her three young sons with their father, Betty ran through a series of jobs, spending her wages on fancy clothes and sports cars. But her life changed when she applied for a nursing position at the newly opened Humana

Hospital–Huntsville and discovered her vocation.

She enrolled at the University of Alabama and within three years had qualified as a registered nurse, specializing in kidney dialysis. Working hard during the day and playing even harder at night, Betty had numerous affairs and dabbled in alcohol and cocaine. The once shy, introverted girl now craved an exciting life in the fast-track, telling friends that she wanted to marry a rich doctor who would take care of her.

As Betty devoted herself to having fun, Peggy settled down to a quiet family life, becoming a first-grade teacher in an elementary school. Money was tight and, in addition to his job as a teacher, Wayne Lowe spent most evenings and weekends selling household goods door-to-door.

The Lowes became prominent members of their local church, where they were respected for their charitable good deeds. Peggy would go out of her way to care for unmarried mothers, sometimes moving them into her home until they got back on their feet. Ironically, Peggy's love of helping strangers would ultimately prove the twins' downfall.

Jack Wray Wilson was born into poverty in a Chicago slum and grew up as an underdog. The illegitimate son of a single waitress named Caroline English, he never knew his real father.

He was adopted as a baby by an eccentric

woman named Wirta Wilson, who collected stray infants and gave them a home. To maintain respectability she stuffed a bulky pillow down her dress when she went out, telling neighbors that she was pregnant to account for her growing family.

Jack had a lonely childhood. His adoptive mother had few maternal instincts and could be cruel and sadistic, often whipping her children if they misbehaved. The frail young boy was often bullied by the neighboring children, who considered him a freak and a misfit. When the insecure child became nervous, he would pick his nose, a habit that stayed with him for the rest of his life.

The young man seemed driven to succeed and rise above his deprived childhood. A natural loner who didn't have a friend in the world, Jack Wilson cut a sad, bedraggled figure with his badly-fitting second-hand clothes. He devoted himself to books and learning, gaining a place two years early in Occidental College. After graduation he found a bookkeeping job, working all hours of the day and night to better himself.

Every night after work he would spend hours in the Occidental University library, often studying past midnight. He developed a passionate interest in optics and began devouring everything he could find on eye diseases. Inevitably, the idealistic young man decided to become an ophthalmologist, so he could help people see properly.

While he was a student at the University of Tennessee Medical School in Memphis, Jack Wilson was diagnosed as suffering from Crohn's disease, which attacks the small intestine. Since childhood, Jack had suffered from chronic diarrhea, fevers and cramps but had stoically refused to seek treatment. Now doctors told him that the only treatment for the disease, which can lie dormant for long periods, was an operation to remove the affected parts of the intestine. As the disease was in remission at the time, he decided not to have the operation unless it got worse.

At Memphis State he met and fell in love with a fellow student named Julia Kelly. The shy young doctor could hardly believe any woman would find him attractive. But the pretty, slender brunette responded to his awkward advances and they were soon married with a child on the way.

It was with a new self-confidence that Dr. Jack Wilson moved to Birmingham, Alabama, with Julia to begin an ophthalmology internship at Charity Hospital. But by the time he set up practice in Huntsville in 1968 the marriage was on the rocks, the victim of Dr. Wilson's relentless work schedule, which left little time for his wife and child.

Even when he was temporarily sidelined with a recurrence of his Crohn's disease, and agreed to undergo the operation to shorten his intestine, he was soon back at his desk working even harder than before to build his practice.

Dr. Wilson took an unconventional attitude to his work, often treating patients for nothing if they couldn't afford his fees. With a knowing wink, he would tell his nurse to put a needy patient "on our hundred-year plan." Before performing eye operations he would pray with patients and his sincerity and happy-go-lucky attitude made his practice thrive.

In 1976, Julia finally left him, taking their two sons and another they had adopted. When his marriage broke up, Dr. Wilson's life fell into a tailspin as he retreated into work, moving into a cheap studio apartment with no furniture except a mattress.

At just thirty-three, Jack Wilson felt that he was a miserable failure and sank into a deep depression.

It was at this vulnerable time that Betty Wilson came into his life when they met during an emergency operation at Huntsville's Humana Hospital. The socially aspiring young nurse was immediately attracted to the eligible rising young doctor, whom she saw as a misdirected man with the potential to succeed.

She immediately asked him out on a date and, just nine months after his divorce in 1977, they were married. In the early years of their marriage Jack Wilson was quite happy for Betty to party at nights while he put in even longer hours at his practice.

His hard work paid off after the introduction of Medicaid, which ensured that the government subsidized his poorer patients instead of him. Now his practice began to take off and soon he was grossing more than a million dollars a year.

Almost overnight the Wilsons became millionaires and Betty encouraged their entree into Huntsville society. They were soon highly sought after by hostesses, who felt that the doctor's wacky sense of humor and eccentricities enlivened their parties.

In keeping with their new status in society, Betty encouraged Jack to buy a lavish house in Boulder City, one of the most exclusive sections of town. The expensive two-story home was perched in a lush wooded lot overlooking Huntsville and boasted an Olympic-sized pool.

Betty Wilson finally had everything she had ever wanted in life as her generous husband overindulged her with new cars, furs, jewels and expensive cosmetic surgery. She even persuaded Jack to set her up in the fashion business, and began traveling all over the world searching for clothes to sell in her Huntsville boutique.

Now drinking harder than ever, Betty wallowed in her new millionaire's lifestyle and loved to boast about it. ''She'd brag about how smart she was,'' says Alisa West, a close friend at the time. "She loved to show off her furs, her burgundy Mercedes convertible and her diamond rings."

But in 1982 Jack's Crohn's disease worsened and he decided to have the rest of his intestines removed, although it meant wearing a colostomy bag for the rest of his life. The radical operation left the doctor impotent and the Wilsons started sleeping in different bedrooms and virtually leading separate lives.

Betty was now drinking so heavily that she began having blackouts where she'd turn on Jack in public, calling him "an asshole." During drinking bouts she would cruelly humiliate him by storming into his bedroom, ripping off the bedclothes and screaming: "You horrible little shitbag! I hate you, I hate you!"

She embarked on a series of one-night stands with strangers she met at parties and would later boast of her sexual exploits to Jack, who would pitifully reply, "It's just sex, Betty."

Finally, Jack decided he couldn't take Betty's affairs any longer and came up with a plan to rekindle their long-dead sexual relationship. One night he came home in unusually good spirits, announcing that he'd bought a vacuum device to allow him to achieve erection.

Betty agreed to give it a try and everything went fine at the beginning, with the device working perfectly. But in the midst of their love-making his colostomy bag came dislodged, covering them both in excrement.

Running from the bedroom in disgust Betty screamed out "Shitbag!" as she rushed into the shower. If their marriage had been strained before, it was now at the breaking point.

Betty Wilson now seemed to be going off the rails. Every day, in the midst of another hangover, Betty called her twin Peggy for marital advice. Patiently, Peggy would listen to Betty's tales of woe about her unhappy marriage and urge her to give up drinking and get her life back on track.

Ironically, when Betty finally joined Alcoholics Anonymous, things went from bad to worse. Attending meetings in her favorite mink coat, Betty told self-pitying stories about her unhappy childhood and growing up in the shadow of Peggy, all of which she taped on a cassette recorder. She also astonished members with her scathing attacks on Dr. Wilson.

"He's a short little shitbag," she said during one luncheon meeting. "The house stinks because he won't take care of the goddamned thing."

The twelve-step program worked for Betty, who stayed on the wagon, attending several A.A. meetings daily and even giving talks on alcoholism to local groups.

But besides sobriety, the meetings also provided her with a new way to meet men and satisfy her sexual lust. She took a series of regular lovers, including several handsome

African-American businessmen who were also looking for no-strings-attached sexual relationships.

She began inviting one lover, Erroll Fitzpatrick, to her home during the day while her husband was at work. In the course of their passionate five-year affair they spent countless afternoons making love in her elaborate bedroom, while her disapproving maid did the housework downstairs. She even invited Erroll to her parties, where she introduced him to Jack, who happily engaged him in friendly conversation.

Betty Wilson's scandalous love-life was soon an open secret in Huntsville. Many of her fellow A.A. members were unhappy about her loose behavior, feeling that it was an unwanted distraction.

"She played around with other men and wouldn't hesitate to say it," scoffed Alisa West.

By 1986 Betty had decided she wanted out of their marriage but did not want to give up her millionaire lifestyle. She told her friend Brenda Cerha, whose own husband had recently committed suicide, that she wanted her husband dead.

"[Betty] said, 'I want to kill Jack,' " Cerha would later testify. " 'Will you help?' She said she envied me because I had inherited my husband's estate and was young and could do whatever I wanted."

But less than a year later at the twins' twenty-fifth high school class reunion, Betty painted a perfect picture of happiness and contentment. Arriving in her gleaming new Mercedes, bedecked in jewels and furs, Betty was determined to leave an impression, showing just how far she had come since leaving East Gadsden.

While the modest Peggy only listed her address in the reunion program's range of accomplishments, Betty's covered a full page.

Billing herself as the owner of three women's boutiques and a part-time fashion model, Betty complained that her heavy social program left her little time for herself.

"Civic affairs can take up one's time," she wrote. "I have fallen into that hole several times. There have been highs and lows galore, but all in all life has been good to me and my loved ones.

"But my best friend is, as always, my twin Peggy. My husband Jack and I have traveled extensively around the world, but home is my favorite place to be. Heaven save me from sand and salt water."

If Betty Wilson was riding the wave of society, James Dennison White was at the bottom of the ocean floor. A Vietnam veteran who was discharged from the Army suffering from chronic battle fatigue, White was an alcoholic, small-time hustler who did odd jobs for anyone who would employ him.

A father of four children through four ex-wives, White was a small, nervous man with a limp, covered in tattoos and missing his right index finger.

When Peggy Lowe first met him in August 1991 at the Vincent Elementary School where she taught, her heart went out to a needy soul. She gave him part-time work building shelves in her classroom, and listened to his tales of woe about the wives who had abandoned him, and his terrible war experiences in Vietnam.

White would later claim that as they became friends Peggy began to confide that she was unhappily married and encouraged his attentions. He became infatuated with the still-beautiful former beauty queen and started writing her love letters. She in turn responded with affectionate kisses.

According to White, Peggy said she had not slept in the same bed as her husband Wayne for more than five years, as his loud snoring repulsed her.

"She said she cringed every time Wayne looked at her and tried to touch her," James White would later testify. "I asked her why she didn't just leave him, and she said she wished something would happen to Wayne. I said, jokingly, that I knew someone who could arrange it."

But White soon realized that Peggy was

deathly serious about hiring a hit man—the twist was that the intended victim was not Wayne but her twin sister's husband, Dr. Jack Wilson.

Over the next few months Peggy Lowe and James White spent hours on the telephone every day as she enticed him into her murderous web. During one conversation she suddenly admitted that she loved him.

"And I said, 'What?'" recalled White. "And she said, 'I didn't mean to say that, but I do.'"

Eventually, when Peggy Lowe admitted that her sister Betty wanted to get rid of her husband, White told her that he had "connections" who could do the job for $20,000. A few days later Peggy called to say that the price was too high and they agreed on $5,000 to be paid in two installments.

White would later claim that Peggy had closed the deal in April 1992 by summoning him to her house to seduce him, wearing "pretty, pinkish-purple underwear."

The following day she paid White the first installment, telling him to be careful. After leaving the house he went straight to his bank to pay off two loans of more than $1,000 each in cash, depositing a further sum into his checking account.

White was so delighted about his new role as a hired killer that he boasted about it to friends, saying that a "rich bitch" was paying him big money to kill her doctor husband. But nobody really took the drunken handyman very seriously, thinking it was just another of his tall tales.

Over the next few weeks White deliberately stalled for time. Finally he got a telephone call from Peggy telling him that Betty wanted her husband killed before Memorial Day.

"I was told Mrs. Wilson wanted to get the job done," said White, "because they were getting ready to take a trip and [she] couldn't stand the thought of spending a week in the hotel with him."

On May 20th, White returned to Peggy's home where he met Betty Wilson for the first time. After giving him instructions on how to get to Dr. Wilson's office, Betty gave him a .38 caliber pistol to carry out the job.

The following morning White drove to Huntsville high on drink and drugs and staked out Dr. Wilson's office. Deciding that it would be too dangerous to kill him there, he called Betty Wilson to say it would be safer to do it the next day at her house.

Betty told him to go to the nearby Parkway City Mall and meet her at a fast-food restaurant in a couple of hours. There she would give him further instructions.

On her arrival she handed him a paper bag with a hundred-dollar bill inside to cover overnight expenses. She told him to check into the Ramada Inn and call her later. Satisfied that everything was in place to kill her husband, Betty White went out to buy a set of new clothes to celebrate.

On Friday, May 22, Betty Wilson seemed in unusually good spirits as she kissed Jack good-bye, arranging to meet him for lunch so they could discuss their impending trip to Santa Fe. It was a sunny morning as Dr. Wilson, dressed casually in a short-sleeved knit shirt and faded jeans, drove off to work and Betty went for her daily swim in their pool.

At lunchtime Jack Wilson came home for a light lunch with Betty. As she optimistically discussed their second honeymoon trip, Betty kept looking at the expensive new watch that her husband had bought her as a birthday present. She was to pick up her hired killer at the mall and did not want to be late.

After dropping her husband off at his practice at 2 p.m. and kissing him good-bye for the last time, Betty drove her black BMW to the mall parking lot a few blocks away. As she was a few minutes early, she popped into Yielding's Department Store and bought a pair of floral designer tennis shoes.

At 2:30 p.m. Betty arrived back at the parking lot to find White waiting for her. He was already drunk and as she drove him back to Boulder Circle, Betty gave him some last-minute instructions before letting him into her home to wait for her husband.

With an empty afternoon ahead of her, to prepare herself for her upcoming ordeal, Betty drove back to town and booked a session in a tanning salon. Then she went on a shopping expedition, buying lingerie and dresses before attending an early evening Alcoholics Anonymous meeting.

While Betty Wilson amused herself shopping, James White was growing restless as he waited for his victim to return home.

''She certainly is a rich bitch,'' White muttered under his breath as he walked around downstairs, admiring the expensive oriental rugs covering polished hardwood floors, and checked out the silver cups, gold ornaments and fine crystal. Swallowing some more pills, he went upstairs and went into Jack Wilson's bedroom.

Suddenly the telephone rang, jolting him back to reality.

''Shut up!'' he screamed at the phone in anger. When it refused to stop he pulled out his knife and cut the telephone wire. Then, as he lay down on the floor trying to will Dr. Wilson to return so he could get it over with, he fell asleep.

James White was awakened by the sound of the front door opening as the unsuspecting doctor finally came home. But Wilson went out again almost immediately carrying a baseball bat to hammer in a campaign poster for his friend Tim Morgan's upcoming election for district attorney.

White felt a clear rush of adrenaline as he tiptoed out of the doctor's bedroom and over to the stairs to see what was going on.

A few minutes later Doctor Wilson entered the house and took off his shoes to make himself more comfortable. He was glad that Betty wasn't home as he would still have a little time alone to relax and compose himself for the trip.

Suddenly, he heard a noise upstairs and realized that he was not alone in the house. Arming himself with the baseball bat, the frail doctor climbed the stairs to investigate. At the top of the stairs he turned the corner and went into Betty's room, where he thought the noise had come from. Nothing seemed to be untoward as he came out to check the other rooms.

Then, as if from nowhere, James White appeared menacingly in front of him like a dreadful apparition. Shocked by the intruder, Dr. Wilson started shouting and lifted the baseball bat to protect himself.

White leapt forward and grabbed the heavy wooden bat from the far weaker man. Taking careful aim at Dr. Wilson's head, he used all his strength to bring it crashing through the doctor's skull and shattering it like an egg shell.

With blood pouring into his eyes and mouth, the 122-pound Dr. Wilson desperately tried to defend himself and lashed out at White. But before he could connect, White began a frenzied attack, raining a series of ferocious blows across the frail doctor's arms and head with the baseball bat. Again and again in sheer bloodlust White brought the heavy bat crashing down on Dr. Wilson, who sank to the floor, his broken body a bloody pulp.

But still White was not finished. He jumped on the dying doctor and, grasping his throat, tried to choke the life out of him. Then reaching for his knife, he began stabbing Dr. Wilson in the chest and stomach until he was dead.

Breathless from the attack, White looked at the doctor's battered body lying on the floor. Then he ran down the stairs, escaping out the garage door to find Betty Wilson anxiously waiting to drive him away in her BMW.

At 9:30 p.m. Betty Wilson called the Huntsville police department to report her husband's murder, saying that she had arrived home to find him lying in a pool of blood outside her bedroom. Within minutes detectives arrived at the Boulder City house to find her sobbing uncontrollably, as she kept asking who could have done it.

When seasoned Huntsville Police Detective Mickey Brantley arrived later that night, Betty Wilson was near hysterics and was being comforted by neighbors. As he told her her husband was dead, she again broke down sobbing, too distressed to answer his questions.

For the next few days Betty Wilson played

the role of grieving widow to perfection. As shocked family and friends rallied to her side with sympathy, Betty hugged and wept with them during the traditional Southern funeral watch. At the funeral Betty looked elegant in black and went into shock as she stood alone, quietly sobbing by the graveside.

The whole town of Huntsville was stunned by the savage death of the popular doctor, who hadn't an enemy in the world. Homicide detectives soon discounted robbery as the motive, deciding instead that it had all the hallmarks of a crime of passion.

On the Sunday after the murder Betty Wilson was asked by detectives if she had ever had affairs outside her marriage. To their astonishment Betty calmly admitted a string of previous lovers, saying she met most of them at A.A. meetings. She stated matter-of-factly that her husband was impotent and had known all about her extramarital affairs, which often took place in their home.

Dr. Jack Wilson's murder was big news in Huntsville, making front-page newspaper headlines and leading off the television news. In the days after the murder Betty Wilson remained cool, calm and collected as she met her lawyers and advisors to discuss the $6.5 million estate she stood to inherit under a new will the doctor had drawn up just four months earlier.

But James White's big mouth would seal the twins' downfall. A few days before the crime, the friend he'd boasted to about being a hit man had filed a report to another police department. It forewarned that a doctor would be murdered and that there were twins involved. Nobody had taken it seriously at the time but when the report routinely came across Detective Brantley's desk soon after the murder, he immediately left for Vincent to question White.

After initially denying murdering Dr. Wilson, the handyman did acknowledge knowing his sister-in-law Peggy Lowe and wife Betty Wilson. As more and more information came to light, White emerged as the prime suspect. And with the evidence mounting against him, he finally agreed to make a confession in exchange for a life sentence and not the electric chair.

Veteran detectives could hardly believe their ears as they listened to White's incredible tale of how the twins had recruited him to murder the rich doctor for his money. He told Detective Brantley about an affair with Peggy Lowe and the "stolen kisses" they'd shared as they planned the hit.

If Huntsville had been shocked by the murder, the news that the victim's widow and sister-in-law had both been arrested in connection with it rocked the town to its very foundation.

As the town's sympathy for Betty evaporated, anger and disbelief set in. Local newspapers carried lurid, sensational stories about

Betty's sexual exploits and cruel indifference to her sick, devoted husband.

One of Dr. Wilson's friends, who had been an emotional crutch for Betty in the days after the murder, summed up popular opinion, saying, "The very idea that I had hugged her made me feel dirty. I took a bath as soon as I could."

As the middle-aged twin sisters languished in Huntsville Jail—awaiting trial and the possibility of the electric chair—they were branded as "cold-blooded black widows" and "twins from hell."

As she sat in her eighth-floor jail cell, wearing inmate's attire in place of her jewels and expensive designer outfits, Betty Wilson plotted to keep her late husband's money and prevent it going to the children from Jack Wilson's first marriage. She demanded that she receive half of the money immediately, but a judge ruled that she would have to wait until after the murder trial.

Betty and Peggy arrived at the courthouse for their arraignment chained together. There they heard the grim news that the police were seeking the death penalty for capital murder.

While Betty Wilson and James White were denied bail, Peggy Lowe was freed on a $150,000 bond, raised by her First Baptist Church in Vincent, which firmly believed in her innocence. For the next eight months until her trial, Betty Wilson stayed in solitary confinement at Madison County Jail, preparing her defense. Peggy Lowe, who would be tried separately, returned home to Talladega to try and resume her life.

A millionairess, on paper at least, Betty decided she needed the best lawyer money could buy and contacted famed Alabama attorney Bobby Lee Cook to defend her. The gentlemanly Southern attorney, reputed to be the model for the hit television series *Matlock*, starring Andy Griffith, readily agreed to take her case, even waiving his fee until after the trial.

A veteran of more than three hundred murder cases, the noted lawyer, who favors seersucker suits in court, said that he took the case because it was a "strange-type killing" with the added attraction of a doctor and his wife. "Mrs. Wilson is a nice, charming lady who did not kill her husband," he told reporters.

The "Alabama Twins" murder case, as it was now known, had become so infamous that a judge agreed to move Betty Wilson's trial 150 miles south to Tuscaloosa, to find a more impartial jury. The tiny agricultural and mining town was a throwback to the old South and probably the only place in Alabama where few people had heard about Dr. Wilson's brutal murder.

Betty Wilson's trial opened on Tuesday, February 23, 1993. After spending almost nine months in jail, she had a complete makeover to create a favorable impression on the jury. The previous Saturday her personal hairdresser had driven down from Huntsville to cut her hair fashionably short and she had ordered a brand-new wardrobe for the trial.

When she made her court entrance, Betty looked more suitably dressed for a high society party than a trial for her life. She wore a smartly cut houndstooth suit and her make-up had been expertly applied by a local beautician.

In his opening argument State Prosecutor Jimmy Fry set the scene by painting a damning picture of a woman consumed with lust and greed, who would stop at nothing to get her husband's fortune and live the good life.

"She is a vain, selfish woman obsessed with her own image and self-appearance," he told the jury. "There was a secret Betty Wilson who took money from her husband without him knowing it and she had lovers that she took into the house he gave her."

The following day James White took the stand and described how his infatuation with Peggy Lowe had driven him to murder. Claiming that he had had sex with Peggy the day before he received his first half of the money, White said that he killed Dr. Wilson out of love.

"[Peggy] is the type of person I dreamed of being with since high school," said the handyman. "She was a higher type society person than I was."

White said that he had planned to strangle the doctor with a rope, but Dr. Wilson had surprised him with the baseball bat and he'd panicked, beating him to death.

In his cross-examination, Betty Wilson's celebrity lawyer Bobby Lee Cook accused White of being a "great big liar," claiming that his client had never even met him.

"How can we tell you're lying?" asked Cook scathingly. "When you open your mouth."

The following Monday accused murderess Peggy Lowe dramatically took the stand to defend her twin sister. In riveting testimony she denied ever having an affair with James White, claiming that she had only given him work out of pity.

"Our family is our life," she said, refuting White's claim that she had an unhappy marriage. "Just the center of our universe."

Four days later, on March 3, Betty Wilson was convicted of arranging the murder of her husband in a plot with her twin sister to inherit his $6.5 million estate. As the verdict was read the middle-aged socialite sat impassively, knowing that she now faced the electric chair.

But an hour later she was spared death when Judge Thomas Younger sentenced her to life in prison without parole, after her step-children intervened to plead for mercy.

"[They decided] to be merciful to someone who had shown no mercy," Prosecutor Fry told reporters outside the courthouse.

As Betty Wilson prepared to spend the rest of her life behind bars at the Julia Tutweiler Prison for Women, her twin Peggy Lowe entered the spotlight with her own murder trial in September, which would be held in Montgomery.

On the first day of jury selection, scores of Peggy Lowe's friends and members of her church paraded outside the Montgomery courthouse to demonstrate their belief in her innocence. The self-named ''Peggy's Posse'' waved placards and flags in her defense.

Peggy Lowe's public-relations campaign, combined with a string of solid testimonials from her husband and members of their church, proved highly effective. In an astonishing turn of events the Montgomery jury acquitted her on all counts.

With tears of joy streaming down her face Peggy pledged to fight for her twin's freedom.

''Betty, I love you,'' she cried. ''We are coming to get you.''

On January 17th, 1997, the Alabama Supreme Court upheld Betty Wilson's conviction, even though three years earlier, before her sister's acquittal, White had recanted his accusations and confession. She was denied a new trial, and will probably spend the rest of her life in jail.

Five

THE TWINS FROM HELL

"Ladybug, ladybug, fly away home, Your house is on fire, and your children will burn"
—Anonymous Nursery Rhyme

A warm breeze whipped off Wolverine Lake, through the expensive lakefront properties and onto Lucielle Street, where it swayed the colored lights and ornaments on the Christmas trees in the front gardens. Although it was the second week of December, the heavy snows that by now usually engulfed the tiny Michigan village, and stayed until spring, had still not arrived.

It was so warm that retired laborer Kendall Craig, Jr., and his wife Elsa were sweating as they carried heavy bags of clean laundry along the lake path to their house.

"It doesn't seem right being in shirtsleeves with Christmas just around the corner," said Kendall, who had lived in Wolverine Lake all of his life, and remembered when it had been marshland. "Can't remember it being so warm this time of the year."

Since retiring from the auto plant in Detroit, Kendall had settled into an easy routine. Mornings were spent helping Elsa with the chores around the house. Then he would slip away to the lake to fish, before meeting his friends in the Big Apple Diner.

That Monday morning they had gotten off to a late start and Kendall just wanted to get home, collect his fishing rod and go to his favorite secluded spot on the edge of Wolverine Lake.

But as he and Elsa walked through the over-grown yard separating the exclusive Wolverine Drive from the blue-collar Lucielle Street, he noticed white steam coming off #65, the house directly across the road from his own. As he came nearer, a thick band of black smoke rose over the large front-porch area.

"Christ! I think that house is on fire!" said Elsa, as she too saw the smoke rising over the blue, single-story wooden house. "Isn't that where those twins live with the little boy who runs around butt-naked all the time?"

Without another word, Kendall dropped his laundry bag and began running toward the house. The smoke was getting thicker and thicker as it poured out of the front door onto the porch.

Running through the ditch into the large front garden to the big oak tree by the porch, Kendall began screaming for help as a huge cloud of black smoke totally obscured the porch from view.

All of a sudden front doors were opening everywhere as other anxious neighbors rushed out to investigate the fire. As Kendall reached the front porch, his neighbor, Denise Childs, came running up behind him, yelling for help. By now the smoke was so thick that it completely covered the whole front of the house.

Although he couldn't see them, Kendall could distinctly hear women's voices coming from the smoke-filled porch. The women appeared to be discussing something, and Kendall couldn't make out what they were saying, but the calmness in their voices reassured him that everything must be under control and there was nothing to worry about.

Nevertheless, as he stared at the smoke-filled house his gut told him that something was dreadfully wrong. It just didn't add up that the voices could be so unconcerned about such a raging fire.

Suddenly the smoke cleared a little and Kendall recognized Gretchen Graham and her twin sister, Gloria Franklin, huddled in the doorway, talking.

"I yelled at them to get out of there," Kendall would later remember, "and before they came out, I overheard one tell the other, 'We have to stick together on our story when we talk to the police or we'll both go to jail.'"

"Are you okay?" screamed Kendall, surprising the sisters, who seemed embarrassed that they had been overheard. They looked at each other sheepishly, like children caught doing something wrong.

Then the dark-haired, heavyset twins calmly walked toward him through the smoke. Although it was midday, Gloria was still in her nightgown while her sister Gretchen was barefoot. Both twins had strange blank expressions on their faces.

Kendall was amazed at how composed and unconcerned they appeared. Then, almost casually, as if as an afterthought, Gretchen said, "We've got a kid in here."

It was at that point that a menacing burst of flame shot out from behind the front door.

"Shawn!" screamed Gloria's mother-in-law, Mary Franklin, who lived next door.

Kendall felt sick to his stomach as he remembered the half-naked little mulatto boy and instantly knew that anyone left inside the house would never get out alive.

Three months earlier, in August 1989, Gretchen Ann Graham had come to Wolverine Lake with her son Shawn to live with her twin sister, Gloria Franklin, and her husband Donald. The thirty-seven-year-old single mother had fallen on hard times and her twin had taken pity on her, agreeing to put a roof over her head and help look after her three-year-old son.

The identical twin sisters were born on October 10, 1952, and seemed to live in a world of their own from the very beginning. Their father was a successful businessman in Union

Lake, Michigan, and their mother was a house-wife.

They grew up in a respectable middle-class home, but had a difficult childhood as their father was an alcoholic and often came home drunk, ordering them to their rooms. Gloria was always the stronger of the twins, looking after her sister and helping her out of the many scrapes she got into as she grew up.

At school the overweight, rather plain-looking twins found themselves near the bottom of the class. They were such slow learners that they were placed in special schools so they could get specialized help.

As a teenager Gloria preferred staying at home and was far less rebellious than her wilder twin sister, who would do anything for kicks. Gretchen moved with a fast crowd, experimenting early with drugs and sex. The pudgy girl with dark lanky hair frequently skipped school with her friends, often disappearing for days at a time.

After leaving school the sisters' lives took separate paths. Gloria married an auto mechanic, Donald Franklin, and settled down in the Detroit suburb of Wolverine Lake to raise a family. Gretchen moved to Waterford, Michigan, where her life became a revolving door of boyfriends and menial jobs to make ends meet.

In her mid-twenties, she had a short-lived marriage to an abusive husband, leaving him after he locked her out of the house late one night. Then she got a job as a dishwasher in a diner and started dating a fellow employee named Mark Graham, who was six years younger.

They married in 1979 and Gretchen attempted to settle down in a smart Detroit suburb. But a few months later she developed a heart murmur and couldn't work, so they were forced to move to low-income housing, with Mark the only breadwinner.

A year later Mark had had enough and divorced Gretchen, saying that he couldn't handle her constant bad moods. Years later, looking back on the marriage, he would remember Gretchen as being a little peculiar and always trying to dupe him out of money.

"Gretchen was like a kid," he recalled. "She needed to be told what to do."

After the divorce Gretchen's life took a sharp, downward turn. She became a prostitute, working the mean streets of Detroit and becoming addicted to hard drugs. Without the good looks of a high-class hooker, Gretchen walked the red-light area of Grand Boulevard and Woodward at night, picking up tricks to pay for her habit.

By her early thirties, Gretchen was floundering with little hope of getting her life back on track. Every time life got too bad she called her sister Gloria, who now had three children, asking for money and advice.

In late 1984 Gretchen became pregnant after

a single encounter with an Afro-American client and everything changed. Against all the
odds she decided to have the baby, seeing it as
an opportunity to start a new life as a mother
and finally get off the streets.

Shawn Michael Graham was born on July 28,
1985, in Botsford Hospital, Farm Hills, Michigan. He was a chubby baby and Gretchen felt
ambivalent toward him. Her own parents felt
ashamed of their new grandson, refusing to accept him because he was half black. When
Gretchen sent her mother a picture of Shawn,
it was returned.

Gretchen had few natural maternal instincts
and did not know how to care for Shawn. It
was the first time in her life that she had had
any real responsibility for another person and
she found it impossible. Every time Gretchen
looked at Shawn, he reminded her of her old,
sordid life as a prostitute, and she began to re-
sent him.

When Shawn was a few months old,
Gretchen moved in with her best friend, Janet
Libtow, and her live-in boyfriend, Raymond
Lee Jensen. The couple were shocked by
Gretchen's apparent disinterest in Shawn and
her total lack of parenting skills.

She hardly fed or clothed him and never
bothered with toilet training or encouraging
Shawn to talk. By the time Shawn was four he
was running wild at Janet's house, desperately

Demented twin doctors Cyril (*left*) and Stewart Marcus had the medical world at their feet in this 1954 class photograph when they were students at the State University of New York's College of Medicine. (*AP/Wide World*)

The Marcus twins lived and died together in this luxury Sutton Terrace apartment block on Manhattan's swanky Upper East Side. (*John Glatt*)

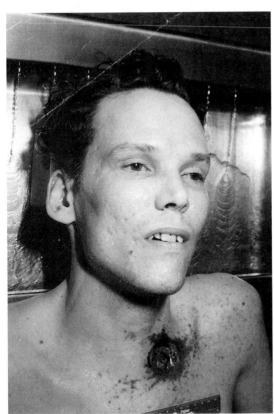

Greg Henry took a fatal shotgun wound to his chest after pushing his twin brother Jeff too far during a drunken argument. (*Douglas County District Attorney's Office*)

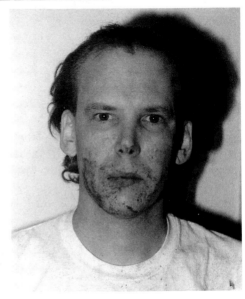

Georgia police photographed Jeff Henry still covered in his twin brother Greg's blood just hours after the murder. (*Douglas County District Attorney's Office*)

Jeff Henry still had his twin brother's blood on his hands when he was arrested for his murder. (*Douglas County District Attorney's Office*)

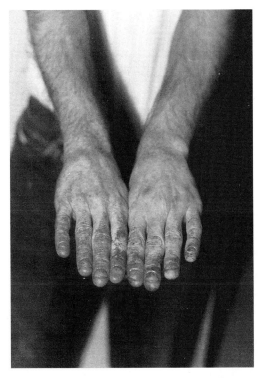

The Sweetwater Creek, Georgia, apartment where the Henry twins lived. (*Douglas County District Attorney's Office*)

As infants, Tim (*left*)
and Todd Nicholson
were as alike as
two peas in a pod.
(*Tim Nicholson*)

When they were
eleven, the Nicholson
twins moved to Florida
with their mother,
Roberta. (*Tim Nicholson*)

Todd (*left*) and Tim Nicholson
with their father Edward in
Costa Rica. (*Tim Nicholson*)

In 1953 Tim (*left*) and Todd (*far right*) delighted in being army cadets and carrying rifles.
(*Tim Nicholson*)

The Nicholson twins seemed the perfect all-American rich kids— until one murdered the other.
(*Tim Nicholson*)

The Nicholson twins pose proudly in the parking lot of Tim's Baldwin Arms apartment building. Soon afterwards Tim (*left*) would kill his twin brother. (*Tim Nicholson*)

Tim Nicholson with his pet ocelot in 1963, a year before he gunned down his twin brother Todd. (*Tim Nicholson*)

Notorious twin gangsters Ronnie (*left*) and Reggie Kray were heartbroken at the London funeral of their beloved mother Violet in 1982. Serving murder sentences at the time, they were given special dispensation to attend. (*AP/Wide World*)

Beautiful Gina Han enters a Santa Ana, CA courtroom in handcuffs, accused of conspiring to murder her twin sister, Sunny.
(*AP/Wide World*)

(*Left*) Sunny Han testified in court on behalf of her twin sister Gina, who was accused of plotting her murder with two accomplices.
(*AP/Wide World*)

(*Right*) Gina Han tried to murder her twin sister, Sunny, blaming her for calling the police and having her jailed for theft. (*AP/Wide World*)

A dramatic moment as Sunny Han breaks down on the witness stand and has to be rushed to the hospital after taking an overdose of sleeping pills during her twin sister's trial. (*AP/Wide World*)

(*Left*) The convicted Gina Han with her defense attorney Roger Alexander. (*AP/Wide World*)

Evil twin Gina Han is now serving a 26-year jail sentence for attempting to murder her sister, Sunny. (*AP/Wide World*)

craving attention. As he had received no potty training, he would regularly mess his pants and received a stiff spanking from his mother as punishment. Janet felt so sorry for the good-natured, playful little boy that she took care of him herself, forming the deep mother's bond that Gretchen was unable to.

"Sean called Janet 'Mom' and referred to his real mother by her name, 'Gretchen,' " remembered Jensen. "She just didn't care for Shawn."

"Gretchen always said that Shawn was in the way of her life," said Janet Libtow. "She never gave Shawn good care."

In August 1989, Gretchen stormed out of the house, after an argument with Libtow that turned violent, leaving Shawn behind. She stayed with a friend named Butch Cathy at the nearby Botsford Apartments, breaking off all contact with Janet and Shawn.

After two days of not hearing from Gretchen, Janet called Protective Services and asked to adopt Shawn. But she was told that she must return Shawn to his real mother. By the time she reluctantly gave him back, Gretchen had decided to move to Wolverine Lake with her twin sister Gloria's family.

Once an affluent suburb of Detroit, the village of Wolverine Lake was a study in contrasts. Lying on marshy swampland, the village became habitable in the 1920s after a special construction project dammed up its network of lakes to form one big one. In the 1930s the Wolverine Lake area was lower-working-class, providing cheap homes to auto workers who had migrated from the Appalachian Mountains in search of work.

But as America's motor industry flourished, Metro Detroit pushed its way out from the river, making Oakland County—which contained Wolverine Lake—the richest area in Michigan.

By the late 1950s, well-heeled Detroiters flocked to Wolverine Lake, building expensive homes on the scenic lakefront, rubbing shoulders with the hillbilly types who were firmly entrenched a few blocks away.

When Donald Franklin married Gloria in the early 1970s, the young couple settled down one block away from the river, on shabby, modest Lucielle Street, two doors away from his mother, Mary Alice Franklin.

Donald worked as a mechanic at the Union 76 service station at the junction of Decker and Pontiac Trail Roads, while Gloria washed dishes at the Big Apple Diner.

In 1974, Donald and Gloria Franklin had a son, Gary, followed by a second boy, Joey, four years later, and a daughter, Julie, born in 1979.

Wolverine Lake was typical of thousands of small communities throughout the length and breadth of America. With a population of 6,000, everybody knew everybody else. And sooner or later, most came to the Big Apple Diner.

The twenty-four-hour diner was the community hub of Wolverine Lake, where you could always find the latest gossip. Workers flocked there for breakfast before driving off to the auto plants in Detroit, returning late at night after the bars closed for coffee and donuts.

The Franklins were known as a decent, hard-working family and well-respected by their neighbors. Their three children were always immaculately dressed and did well at school, never getting into any trouble.

Donald Franklin was a familiar figure in Wolverine Lake with his steel glasses, receding hair and pencil-thin mustache. Although he liked to project the image of the God-fearing family man with a deep social conscience, the truth would turn out to be different.

When Gretchen and Shawn Graham arrived that summer, it was clear from the onset that the young half-caste did not fit into the pattern of life in Wolverine Lake. The Franklins saw him as an embarrassment, sectioning him off from the rest of their children.

Shawn and his mother slept in a small closet, which had been converted into a bedroom with its own lavatory, at the back of the house. And while Gretchen and Shawn lived in cramped conditions, Donald and Gloria Franklin occupied a luxurious master bedroom and their three children all had their own bedrooms in the basement.

To the curious four-year-old, the new home seemed like a palace. He immediately started exploring it, opening doors to the various rooms and climbing all over the furniture. Before long he had angered Donald Franklin by accidentally smashing his model collection, and causing other minor damage.

Franklin put Shawn on probation and told Gretchen they would have to leave if Shawn didn't start to behave. To try and rein in the naturally adventurous little boy, he affixed a slide bolt to Gretchen and Shawn's living quarters, so he could be locked up whenever the family didn't want him around.

Franklin also placed a large stove that was too tall for Shawn to climb over across another doorway access, creating a virtual prison. Shawn would be caged for hours at a time, whenever it was felt necessary.

Gretchen was working with Gloria at the Big Apple Diner, washing dishes from midnight until 8 a.m. She loved her new life and had even embarked on a sexual relationship with her brother-in-law with the full knowledge, albeit grudging approval, of her twin sister.

Gloria had been furious when her elder son found out about the relationship and complained to her. When she confronted her husband about sleeping with her twin sister, he assured her that it was all right, as it was family.

He then threatened to leave, saying that he had to have both sisters or none. Without any other means of support Gloria was forced to turn a blind eye to the affair.

Gretchen's life revolved around the Big Apple Diner where she struck up a close friendship with a young twenty-three-year-old dishwasher named Christopher Weymers, who had a criminal record. The two found a kinship, occasionally smoking marijuana joints outside the diner to make the all-night shift pass a little faster. After work Weymers would drive her back to Lucielle Street in return for some gas money.

For the first time in her life Gretchen seemed to have a purpose in life. She was popular at the diner and loved to chat and share a joke with the customers. After finishing work at 8 a.m., she would join them in the main dining area for breakfast, before going home to sleep on the living room couch.

The only dark cloud on her horizon was Shawn, who was now becoming more mischievous than ever. Two months after they moved in, Gretchen called her estranged friend Janet Libtow for help. She begged her to adopt Shawn and raise him, saying that she was scared of being evicted by the Franklins.

''She told me that Shawn was in the way,'' Libtow remembered. ''She couldn't do what she wanted to do so she asked me to raise him.''

As Libtow had just been released from the hospital, she told Gretchen that she was not well enough to take on the added responsibility of Shawn.

It was a fateful decision that she would later come to regret.

By November 1989, the sisters had decided to cage Shawn every morning when they returned from work so they could sleep. He would remain locked in his prison for hours until he was finally released when they woke up.

The wild little boy was now causing quite a stir in the neighborhood. During a cold snap that fall he was seen playing half-naked in the front garden, which he used as a toilet in full view of the neighbors. He was allowed to run around barefoot outside and was always causing trouble, getting into the neighboring gardens.

It became common knowledge that there were double standards of care for the four children in the house. One for the three Franklins, who were well–cared for and well-loved, and one for Shawn Graham, who was treated little better than the family's pet cat, Fluffy, who was his only friend.

Things went from bad to worse after Shawn found a lighter and set fire to his bedroom curtains. Although Donald Franklin managed to extinguish the blaze before any real damage was done, Shawn was locked up as punishment.

A furious Franklin threatened to kick him out again. He warned the rest of the family to be careful to place all lighters and matches out of Shawn's reach, on a high shelf over the stove. To emphasize the lesson, Gretchen forced Shawn's fingers over a lighted match, to teach him about the dangers of fire.

Around that time welfare workers from the Department of Social Security arrived at the Franklin house to investigate complaints that Shawn was being ill-treated. Although they found heavy bruising on the boy's leg, they accepted Donald Franklin's explanation that Shawn had fallen down on the playground.

By early December, Gretchen had tired of her affair with Franklin, which had been causing tension in the house. She was fed up with his repeated demands for sex and complained to friends about his unwanted attentions. "There are times when I wish that Don would just leave me alone," she told them. "It's kind of forcing me."

On Saturday, December 9, Shawn stole a yellow Bic lighter and carefully hid it in his room. When Gretchen discovered it missing she told Donald Franklin, who suspected Shawn and ordered the house "torn apart" until it was found.

But Sean was too clever for them and it stayed hidden. The little boy was delighted by his new toy. He loved flicking the top and seeing the beautiful yellow flames dance around.

Somehow it had a magical power that could

scare grown-ups and make them mad. Now when they imprisoned him he would have a new friend to play with.

At 7 a.m. on Monday, December 11, Gretchen Graham awoke from the couch where she had slept and went into the kitchen. She had not worked the previous night shift and, feeling unusually refreshed for so early in the morning, looked forward to a leisurely day.

She found the three Franklin children eating breakfast with Gloria, who was preparing them for school. For once, she noticed, Shawn was sitting on the floor quietly playing with his Matchbox cars, and not causing trouble. After asking her son Joey to look after Shawn, she and Gloria drove to the Big Apple Diner for breakfast.

Half an hour later they returned to pick up Shawn and drive into the village. Gloria needed to buy a money order from the Anchor Drug Store and pick up some groceries. As Gloria bought the money order, Gretchen took Shawn to the other side of the store to look at the candy display.

"Shawn wanted a stuff [sic] animal," Gretchen would recall later. "I said, 'No, son. I don't have the money.' "

When Shawn burst into tears, Gretchen carried him out and put him in the car. Then Gloria returned, announcing that she needed to go to the Union 76 service station so her husband could fix her broken windshield wiper. An hour later they returned to the house, leaving Shawn to play while they watched television.

At about 10:30 a.m. Gretchen's friend Chris Weymers arrived to collect some money he was owed. After opening the front door, Gretchen told him to wait outside while she found her purse. As he watched through the open door he saw a tearful Shawn suddenly burst half-naked into the living room with Gretchen in hot pursuit.

"She was yelling, 'Come here, you little motherfucker!'" Weymers would later recall. "I saw Gretchen hit Shawn from behind on his back. He went forward and she grabbed him."

Stunned by what he had seen, Weymers asked Gretchen if she was going to work and left when she said she had the day off.

The twins then settled down on the living room couch to watch the "Sally Jessy Raphael" show. Gloria had undressed and put on a nightgown so she could sleep while Gretchen filled in a job application form.

When Shawn, who had been playing with his toy cars on the floor nearby, announced that he needed the lavatory, Gretchen was angry at being disturbed. After shouting and swearing at him, she took the boy to the bathroom, leaving the door open so she could see what he was doing.

Shawn suddenly dashed out again without doing his business, making Gretchen even madder as she dragged him back to the toilet to finish. Then she returned to the living room and went to sleep in a chair.

Gloria also wanted to sleep, so after giving Shawn a sandwich she took him into his bedroom and left him there with Fluffy for company. Then she locked the door so he couldn't disturb them, returning to the living room where she fell asleep on the couch with the "Sally Jessy Raphael" show playing in the background.

Just before midday, Gloria Franklin awoke to the smell of burning. She looked up from the couch to see smoke coming from the kitchen across from Shawn's bedroom. Coming to her senses and realizing that the house was on fire, she shook Gretchen, who jumped up when she understood what was happening.

Suddenly Shawn started crying for help from the room where he was imprisoned behind the smoke-filled kitchen. The twins looked at each other as if asking the other what to do.

"Where's Shawn?" asked Gretchen, desperation creeping into her voice.

"I locked him up so we could sleep," replied her sister.

A phone was lying on a nearby table just a few feet away from the locked door that separated Shawn from freedom. Gretchen picked up the receiver and started to dial 911 but suddenly stopped, putting it down again as she heard her son's desperate screaming.

In a momentary flash of understanding between the twins, each knew exactly what the other was thinking. It would have been simple for them to unlock the door and rescue Shawn. But on the other hand, he had started the fire and it could be the solution to their problems.

If Shawn were to die in the fire everyone's life would be so much easier. After all, he was nothing but trouble and who would miss him anyway?

Their minds were made up by the time Gloria feebly asked Gretchen if she was going to unlock the door and let him out.

"No. It's better for him to die," replied Gretchen coldly, as she watched the thick black smoke pouring out from Shawn's prison. Gloria shrugged her shoulders in silent agreement, leading her sister across the living room to the front door, which they opened just a crack for fresh air.

Then they waited for the boy to burn to death, listening to his blood-curdling whimpers.

It was a full five minutes before they were certain that Shawn was dead. They would later remember hearing him take his last breath as the kitchen burst into flames.

At 12:02 p.m. Gretchen finally picked up the phone and dialed 911 to report the fire, knowing full well that she had rid herself of her burdensome son.

The twins felt a strange calm as they ventured out of the burning house to the front porch to discuss their next move. It wouldn't be long before the fire trucks arrived, so they began to formulate a plan. They knew they would have to explain why Shawn had perished while they had escaped.

Standing on the porch as the house burned behind them, they worked out a scenario to tell the police. Gretchen would say that she'd gone back into the house to rescue the boy but had been beaten back by the thick smoke.

Then the twins hugged each other as they vowed to stick together so they wouldn't go to jail.

Detective Chris Helgert had enjoyed a long and distinguished career working for the Arson Squad at the Highland Park Police Department in central Detroit. It was big-city action and he had worked his way up to the position of Chief. But after nine years investigating arson homicides, he had moved to Wolverine Lake, where life was quieter and a little more laid-back.

On Monday, December 11, Detective Helgert spent the morning in Flint on business. Arriving back in Wolverine Lake in the early afternoon, he was immediately summoned to a major fire at 652 Lucielle Street.

By the time he arrived the fire was out and he went straight into the smoldering remains of the single-story wooden house. There he found his friend, Deputy Jim Lehtola, leading other officers from the Oakland County Sheriff's Department in a preliminary investigation.

Helgert and Lehtola had known each other for years. They had started their careers together as teenage volunteer firefighters before joining the Highland Park Arson Squad. Now they were both nationally recognized arson investigators and acknowledged fire experts.

Deputy Lehtola quickly briefed Helgert on the fire, which had claimed the life of little Shawn Graham. Lehtola's team had just found the boy dead in a bath in the fetal position, along with the charred remains of a cat. Shawn's mother and aunt had already been questioned at a neighbor's house and their stories did not add up.

He told Helgert that although the sisters' explanations of the fire were mainly consistent, there were minor discrepancies that sounded alarm bells in his head.

Gretchen and Gloria both claimed that they were filling out job applications while Shawn was playing somewhere in the house. They suddenly saw a big wall of fire come from the kitchen and ran out of the building in fear for their lives.

"I went back in because my son was [inside]," Gretchen had tearfully told detectives. "I was beaten back by the thick smoke. I was crying because my son was still in the house."

Gloria readily backed up her twin sister's

claim of having gone back inside the burning house to save Shawn.

"That scenario was impossible," explained Detective Helgert. "And then we physically read the fire and looked at the damage and it just did not mesh with what they told us."

Suspecting foul play, Helgert and Lehtola immediately launched a meticulous investigation of what remained of the charred house. They worked until the early hours and then returned the following day to complete it.

The two investigators deduced that the fire started in Shawn's closet-bedroom before consuming the hallway and lavatory and entering the kitchen area, which Donald Franklin had blocked off with a stove to contain Shawn. They were convinced that Shawn had started the fire with his lighter and then gotten trapped.

Lehtola and Helgert spent hours carefully sifting through the charred remains of the hallway, closet-bedroom and lavatory where Shawn had perished. At one poignant point they heard little Julie Franklin calling her cat Fluffy for food, and looked down to see his burnt remains.

Their big breakthrough came when they discovered the slide bolt of Shawn's prison door, noticing that it had been in the "closed" position at the time of the fire.

"This established that Shawn Graham's body was locked in a portion of the house from which he was unable to escape," explained Detective Helgert.

The day after the fire an autopsy revealed that Shawn had died of smoke and soot inhalation. Although the cause of death was officially registered, the medical examiner refused to say how he had died, pending further investigation.

In the days following the fire the twins arranged Shawn's burial and organized a memorial service. They moved into Mary Franklin's house two doors away while her son Donald filed a claim for fire insurance from the Prudential, putting the remains of his lot up for sale at $58,000.

Moved by the plight of the now-homeless Franklin family, the village of Wolverine Lake rallied to their cause, starting a collection which raised $3,000 to help them begin again.

Still working the midnight shift at the Big Apple Diner, Gretchen would readily describe the fire, saying that she was devastated by her son's death. Fellow workers noticed how her attitude toward Shawn had changed since his death. Instead of constantly complaining about him, she now talked about him as if he had been a saint.

The sisters may have believed that they had gotten away with murder, but Detective Helgert and Deputy Lehtola vowed to bring them to justice, however long it took.

"I cried myself to sleep more than once during that time," remembered Detective Helgert, who doesn't have any children of his own.

"Most good policemen will tell you that it's not difficult to distance yourself from the whole thing. But in a small community like this you know everybody and it brings it even closer."

The Wolverine Lake Police Department dubbed it "the Shake and Bake Case," developing a simple but highly effective strategy to trap the twins into confessing.

They eased off the pressure for a couple of months to lull the sisters into a false sense of security. Then, using the element of surprise, they planned to requestion each sister separately until they finally cracked.

As soon as Gretchen Graham's old roommate Janet Libtow heard about the fire from a friend, she suspected that Shawn's death had been no accident. Well aware of how Gretchen had despised her son, Janet telephoned her at Mary Franklin's house for answers before going to the police with her suspicions.

"I got a few days off work because of all of this. Life goes on. I can always have another child," Gretchen coldly told Libtow, adding that Gloria and Donald Franklin had told her not to discuss the fire.

But Gretchen was finding it impossible to keep quiet about it. One night after a few drinks she confided in Christopher Weymers during their midnight shift at the Big Apple.

"Gretchen told me that she loved him but he's better off dead so he doesn't have to grow up in this cruel world,'' Weymers would later tell police. ''She said that the kid was locked up in the bathroom at the time of the fire and couldn't get out.''

Almost four months after the blaze, with the twins believing the case was closed, Detective Helgert put his investigation into high gear.

On March 8, 1990, he arrived at the Big Apple Diner after midnight and interviewed Gretchen in an empty office. She admitted arguing with Shawn shortly before the fire and acknowledged for the first time that he had been locked inside the hallway. But she still maintained that she had not been able to save him because of the dense smoke.

A few hours later, Helgert visited Gloria at the nursing home where she was working. He was careful to time it so that Gretchen couldn't brief her sister beforehand. It was during this two-hour interview that Gloria finally confessed that Shawn had been allowed to die and could easily have been saved.

In a written statement she pointed the finger at Gretchen, saying that her twin had ''murdered'' Shawn, deciding that he would be better off dead. When Helgert asked her if she too felt guilty of causing her nephew's death, she replied, ''Yes.''

She then revealed her sister's affair with her husband, adding that Donald Franklin was out grocery-shopping with Gretchen and even now she feared they might be having sex.

"[I'll] find out when I get home and see if there's any groceries in the house," she said.

Now that he had Gloria's signed confession, Helgert brought Gretchen straight into Wolverine Lake Police Station for questioning.

Initially she stuck to her original story without knowing about her sister's confession. But under Helgert's persuasive questioning, she finally broke down and admitted murdering her son. Saying that she had lied up to now because she was "afraid and ashamed" of her actions, a tearful Gretchen made a complete written confession.

"At the time of the fire," she wrote, "when my sister said, 'What about Shawn? Are you going to get him?' I said no because I thought it would be best for Shawn to die.

"Gloria and Don really didn't want Shawn around anyway. So yes I did think at the time of the fire it would be better for Shawn to die."

For the next ten days the twins remained free, as prosecutors obtained warrants to charge them with murder. The village of Wolverine Lake was shocked into disbelief to hear that Gretchen and Gloria were being investigated for the murder of the child.

It had been fifteen years since the last homicide in Wolverine Lake and even Police Chief James R. Davis couldn't recall the name of the youth who had bludgeoned his father to death with a rifle.

Murder was the chief topic of conversation at the Big Apple Diner, where Gretchen still pulled a midnight shift. Opinion squarely sided behind the twins with the feeling that they were being unjustly persecuted by police.

Donald Franklin actively campaigned against Chief Davis' police department, driving around the village in his Ford Pinto sporting a large bumper sticker reading, "WOLVERINE LAKE POLICE ARE CORRUPT."

"The community accused me of harassing these poor twins," remembered Detective Helgert. "Even some of the elected officials were making noises to try and halt our investigation. The extraordinary nature of the crime, filicide by fire, was met with near disbelief by many citizens and more than one member of the public safety committee."

On March 19, 1990, Gretchen Graham and Gloria Franklin were finally arrested for first-degree murder and conspiracy to commit first-degree murder. If convicted, the sisters both faced life in prison without parole. The twins' arrest caused a sensation in Wolverine Lake and the next morning's *Oakland Press* carried it on the front page with the headline, MOM, AUNT ARRESTED IN FIRE DEATH.

In a hastily called press conference, Oakland County Prosecutor Richard Thompson told reporters that the defendants both had the opportunity to save Shawn but had abandoned him to a horrible death.

"Unbelievable," said Thompson. "It's a sad, heart-wrenching situation."

The following day the twins were arraigned for murder with a judge posting their bail bonds at $1 million. That meant that the Franklin family would have to come up with $100,000 each to free them from jail until the trial. Sitting side-by-side looking distraught throughout the arraignment, the overweight twins clasped each other's hands for support.

Donald Franklin told the judge there was no way he could raise the surety as the fire had wiped him out financially. He explained that he was still battling the Prudential to pay out insurance, as they claimed he had not kept his premium payments up to date.

Outside the courtroom, Gloria's mother-in-law, Mary Alice Franklin, accused Detective Helgert of a witch hunt. "You're breaking up a whole household," she screamed. "I don't know what you stand to gain by this."

Her son Donald moved quickly to exercise spin control by giving an exclusive interview to *The Oakland Press*, claiming that the twins were far too stupid to have planned Shawn's murder.

Taking the moral high road against the Wolverine Lake Police Department, the now-admitted adulterer described his family as "close-knit God-fearing people."

He told reporters that the twins were "learning disabled" and would be incapable of knowing how to act in an emergency situation like the fire.

"It's mentally impossible for them to plan a murder," he said. "I don't see how they would have confessed to something they didn't do. They were under so much pressure they could have crumbled and confessed to anything.

"It broke our hearts when it first happened. Now with these charges against Gloria and Gretchen, it's doubly hard."

Then, amazingly, he accused Shawn of being directly responsible for his own death by stealing the cigarette lighter.

"He was four, mischievous and more or less did himself in," declared Franklin.

After a month-long preliminary hearing, the twins were ordered to stand trial on second-degree murder charges after Judge Michael Batchik ruled that the killing was not premeditated.

Both sisters were ashen-faced, their heads bowed in shame, as they were led from court past Gloria's three children, who were crying in the visitors' gallery. They were taken to the Oakland County Jail House to spend the next six months behind bars, preparing for their murder trial.

On Thursday, December 20, 1990, Gretchen Graham and Gloria Franklin both pleaded no contest to second-degree murder charges. After sentencing the twins to prison for eight to forty years, Oakland County Judge Edward Sosnick said that Shawn did not have to die.

"In a better world there would have been a place for this child," he told the sisters. "Someone should have recognized that you couldn't care for this boy."

Choking back tears, both sisters separately addressed the court, still apparently denying responsibility for Shawn's death.

"I loved my son very much—more than my own life," wept Gretchen. "I tried [to save him], but the smoke was so bad, and I failed."

Gloria Franklin was also crying as she pledged her love for Shawn.

"I have three children of my own," she sobbed. "I have to get home and take care of my children."

A few months later Detective Helgert left the Wolverine Lake Police Department, thoroughly disillusioned with the close-knit community that had so ostracized him during the investigation.

Six

SILENCE OF THE TWINS

"We once were two, We two made one We
no more two, Through life be one"

—Izaak Walton

It was an unseasonably warm spring day as
June Gibbons walked slowly through the
cemetery to visit the grave of her twin sister,
Jennifer. Today was their thirty-first birthday
and June had been preparing for weeks, viewing it as the closure of their bizarre twinship.

Since Jennifer had so tragically died, just
hours after the twins' release from serving
twelve years in Britain's notorious Broadmoor
Hospital for the criminally insane, June had finally come to terms with the strange demons
that had wreaked havoc with both their young
lives.

Cutting themselves off from the world as
small children, and speaking only to each other,
the twins' silent pain had finally exploded into
arson, resulting in a life sentence behind bars,
alongside some of England's most hardened
criminals.

As the petite, well-dressed black woman,
sporting dreadlocks, wiped a tear from her eye

and placed a bunch of yellow tulips on the grave, she could hear her dead twin beckoning her over to the other side. But this would be one game that June would refuse to take part in.

Since the age of three, her dominant sister had always called the tune, ordering June to do her evil bidding. For almost thirty years of her life, June Gibbons had felt like a helpless zombie, powerless to disobey. But now that Jennifer was dead and the psychic shackles broken, June had been reborn with her own identity.

And as she walked away from the grave she felt a strange mixture of love and hate for the identical twin who had so cruelly enslaved her.

When she looked back on her life from the vantage point of freedom, June Gibbons would have given anything not to have been born a twin, considering it a curse. Since her birth ten minutes before Jennifer on April 11, 1963, her destructive twinship had brought nothing but misery and unhappiness.

Their Barbados-born father, Aubrey Gibbons, had a successful career as an air flight controller in the Royal Air Force before being posted to England in the early 1960s. Taking his young wife Gloria and two children, Greta and David, the family did the rounds of air force bases around England and Wales.

Aubrey was delighted when June and Jennifer were born. As the eldest of six children himself, the ambitious young immigrant dreamed of a large family, lavishing love and attention on his new twins.

Even as babies Jennifer seemed to dominate her placid twin sister. She was the first to sit up and crawl and bitterly competed with June for their mother's milk.

Nine months after the twins were born, Aubrey was promoted and transferred to Linton, Yorkshire. Looking like identical little dolls, June and Jennifer turned heads when Gloria took them into town, dressed in their identical romper suits.

As infants the twins seemed perfectly normal, happily playing with each other for hours. The first sign that something was wrong came at the age of three, when they both had trouble talking. While most children can already speak in short sentences at that age, the twins' vocabulary was limited to just a few words.

By the time they started school at the age of five, their speech had not improved. As they sat silently at the back of the class, Jennifer and June frustrated their teachers by refusing to communicate with anything more than nods. The only black children in their class, the Gibbons sisters were conspicuous anyway; their silence was misinterpreted by teachers as dissension.

The Gibbons twins were mercilessly bullied by the other children, who saw them as freaks. Soon they began to withdraw from the world, retreating into their twinship as protection against a hostile world. They even refused to speak to their parents at home, becoming more isolated as the years went by.

It was only when they were alone that June and Jennifer would open up and talk. They communicated in a strange high-pitched chatter that only they could understand. And in a deliberate attempt to cut themselves off from the world and become self-sufficient, they had invented their own secret language with its own words and nuances. But when anyone else came into the room they would go silent and stare blankly into space.

"It started as a game," June would explain many years later. "But the longer it went on the more trapped we felt. It went too far and although we longed to be normal we couldn't break out."

In 1974, Aubrey was re-posted to an RAF base at Havorfordwest in the idyllic, rolling hills of West Wales. Although his twin daughters were eleven, he and his wife had never had a single conversation with them. While the rest of the family chatted happily at the dinner table at their new home in Furzy Park, June and Jennifer remained silent, ignoring everyone. Where they would once at least mumble a single-word reply to their parents' questions, they now responded only with frosty silences.

The twins' strange behavior created tension in the Gibbons household, casting an all-pervasive shadow over the family. And when the twins started the Havorfordwest County Secondary School, Aubrey sought the help of an educational psychologist, who reassured him that they would improve as they grew older.

But at their new school things stagnated as the twins retreated further into themselves, appearing like matching space aliens to their teachers and schoolmates.

On the first day of term they lined up in their new school uniforms in the head teacher's study. Standing one in front of the other, they refused to give their names for register. And from then on they arrived each day at school, perfectly groomed, with their long hair in plaits, but stayed as silent as stone statues.

In between classes, June would goose-step exactly ten yards behind Jennifer through the school corridors and onto the playground, while the other children looked on in amazement. They maintained this strange parade throughout the day, never letting down their guard.

Again they were bullied cruelly for their strange behavior by the other children, who found them sinister and unnerving. Things got so bad that the twins were allowed to go home five minutes early to avoid any trouble from their hostile schoolmates at the gate.

The Gibbons girls' hostility permeated the whole school. Their frustrated teachers viewed them as unruly and difficult, and at the age of thirteen they were placed in a remedial class for backward pupils. When the school's medical officer, Dr. John Rees, met the twins during a routine vaccination line-up, he was astonished at their total lack of reaction to the needle.

"They were like zombies," he said. "There was nothing there. It was as if they were in a trance."

When Dr. Rees summoned their parents to school to probe further, he was told that the twins were just shy and never spoke at home. Surprised at Aubrey's reaction and convinced that there might be a medical problem responsible for their silence, Dr. Rees referred them to an expert, who diagnosed them as suffering from a rare mental condition called elective mutism, where a person decides not to talk.

A speech therapist who examined the Gibbons twins at the time saw firsthand how Jennifer had become her sister's psychic jailer. Every time June attempted to speak, her controlling twin would prevent her from doing so.

"I know she was stopping June," said the therapist. "[It was] like extrasensory perception. She sat there with an expressionless gaze but I felt her power. She made all the decisions. June was possessed by her twin."

Up to then June and Jennifer had never caused any trouble at school and were model pupils, except for their refusal to speak. But once they were sent to a special education center to treat their elective mutism, Jennifer led June into a frightening new phase, as they retreated even further. And behind their wall of silence the twins' minds were working faster than ever, erecting an impenetrable wall against the world.

The Eastgate Center for Special Education was situated in a crusty gothic-style Victorian church, eight miles away from their home. During an early visit to the center the two sisters sat side-by-side on a couch sipping tea in perfect unison. Like exact mirror images they would cross and uncross their legs as they slowly brought the tea cups to their mouths like two synchronized swimmers.

During the first week they spoke to no one, appearing to be moving together in slow motion. At lunchtime they would stare at their food, refusing to eat it. Then they would slowly march out of the dining room, one behind the other.

One curious Eastgate teacher secretly left a tape recorder in a room with the twins, to discover if they spoke when alone. Later when it was played back, the teacher was stunned to hear a girlish giggle followed by June's clear voice.

"What can we say?" asked June.

"God knows, God knows," replied Jennifer.

Over the next year the Gibbons twins managed to divide and conquer their teachers. Half the staff wanted to separate them to discover if being apart from her Svengali-like sister would benefit June. The others passionately believed that this would be detrimental to both. It led to heated arguments at case meetings.

Eventually it was decided to split them up. When the girls found out, they were furious, embarking on a sinister campaign to stay together. They began plaguing Eastgate staff members at home with anonymous telephone calls in strange, twangy American accents.

"Good evening. This is the twins," began one of the calls. "We'd like you to know that if you don't separate us, we'll start talking next week!"

When a doctor officially told the girls they were to be parted, Jennifer went berserk. Like a crazed cat she lunged at June with her long nails and scratched her face deeply. Then June leaped forward, grabbed her sister's head and tried to pull her plaits out. It took all the doctor's strength to pry them apart.

Separated for the first time in their lives, the twins' behavior degenerated even further. Pining for her sister, June went on a hunger strike. She became almost catatonic except when she was allowed to telephone Jennifer at lunchtimes. During the daily calls June came alive as she feverishly chattered to her sister in girlish giggles. But as soon as she put the phone down she returned to her former zombie state.

Astonished staff who witnessed the conversations became convinced that Jennifer deliberately kept her sister on a psychic leash, refusing ever to let her go.

"There was something almost mystic about their relationship, like black magic," said one expert who treated them. "I felt June could have been a normal, popular young girl if she had been released from her sister."

After a few months the twins won their battle as their frustrated doctors were forced to admit defeat and reunited them.

At the age of sixteen June and Jennifer Gibbons left school with no qualifications and entered a new phase by retreating into their bedroom. With no chance of ever finding work without talking, they signed on for unemployment. Then they began to invent an elaborate fantasy world with their dolls, helped by their younger sister, Rosie, the only person they would talk to.

Shutting themselves away in their bedroom for days, the silent twins began playing a warped kind of Happy Families, using dolls to act out their fantasies. Over the next few months they invented a strange, sophisticated parallel world. Dreaming up intricate plots, they cast their dolls in life-and-death situations in their private ongoing soap opera.

They even launched their own personal radio station, taking the roles of news anchors, disc jockeys and weather forecasters. But whenever their parents ventured up to the room, they went silent. And Aubrey and Gloria Gibbons never dared try and invade the strange world of illusion the twins now lived in.

For Christmas 1980 the twins both received large red diaries, unleashing a fertile new outlet for their expression.

They decided to become famous writers, enrolling in a creative writing course to learn grammar, punctuation and plot development. They began to study classic literature like Jane Austen, D. H. Lawrence and the Brontë Sisters as inspiration for their own work. Just three weeks after receiving her diary, June began a full-length novel, called *The Pepsi Cola Addict*.

Surprisingly, the teenage mute, with no experience of the outside world, set the novel in Malibu, California, weaving complex themes of unrequited love and homosexuality. Five months later she had finished the manuscript and began sending it off to publishers.

After a string of rejections a vanity house accepted it, demanding $1,500 to cover printing and publishing costs. After much negotiation by the twins, the publisher agreed to accept the money in monthly installments. Jennifer, inspired by her twin sister's success as a published author, immediately embarked on her own novel, called *The Pugilist*.

At the age of eighteen June and Jennifer Gibbons discovered boys. After two years in their bedroom they left to pursue romance in their own strange, inimitable fashion. Since puberty they had deliberately bound their breasts to give themselves boyish appearances. Now they suddenly began to explore their sex appeal with a vengeance, experimenting with make-up and low-cut dresses.

Purchasing a pair of binoculars, they began spying on prospective youths living nearby and mailed anonymous love letters to any they fancied. They also sent away for a book on witchcraft, attempting to harness the power of black magic spells and voodoo dolls as the necessary aids to find boyfriends.

When their spells failed to work, the disillusioned twins decided to take matters into their own hands. They began spending all their unemployment money taking taxis to a nearby American base to track down a serviceman's son whom they'd met at Eastgate. Although the boy had recently returned to America, he had three brothers who were only too happy to meet the twins.

On their first date the boys failed to show up. Undeterred, the girls started breaking into the brothers' house to rifle through their bedrooms in search of souvenirs. One night they were caught by the boys' parents, who were so intrigued by the strange, silent identical twins that they invited them to stay for coffee and meet their sons.

That was the beginning of a wild period of adventure for the girls that would have disastrous results. As they began to date the American boys, the painfully shy twins had to build up their nerves with cigarettes and vodka. Soon the worldly boys had introduced them to marijuana, glue-sniffing and sex.

Over the next few weeks the girls became sex slaves to the handsome fourteen-year-old Chuck, whom they both fancied. Jennifer was the first to lose her virginity, on the steps of a church, watched by her jealous twin sister. A few days later June evened the score by triumphantly losing hers.

The fanciful twins mistook lust for love and fell deeply in love with their underage Casanova. To Chuck and his brothers the girls were a joke, to be treated with contempt when they weren't taking sexual advantage of them. But the more the boys physically slapped and humiliated them, the more deeply the twins fell in love.

When the brothers returned to America with their family without telling them, the twins were devastated and considered suicide. Desperate for love, they began offering their bodies to any boys who would pay attention to them.

Looking for new kicks to satisfy their craving for excitement and danger, they decided to achieve fame and fortune as master criminals.

After months of stealing bicycles and joy-riding around the Welsh countryside, Jennifer and

June wanted to move out of petty crime into the major leagues.

They began by breaking into homes around their housing estate, stealing cakes, stationery and anything else that appealed to them. "My life of crime is going from good to better," wrote Jennifer in her diary, as she planned the twins' next criminal adventure. The previous week they had set fire to a local tennis court, finding the thrill of arson irresistible. Since then they had torched three schools and several offices around the Havorfordwest area.

On Saturday, October 24, 1981, Jennifer and June Gibbons decided to burn down a tractor store near their home. Rain was falling as the twins climbed over the barbed-wire fence surrounding the machine store, smashing a window to gain entrance to the shed housing the tractors and threshing machines. It was pitch-black inside. June lit a match so they could get their bearings as Jennifer led her toward an open office.

To the twins the office, full of expensive office equipment and supplies, was like a treasure trove. After filling up the plastic bags they'd brought with loot, Jennifer began dousing the floor and furniture with gasoline.

As she lit the match, June savored the moment before she dropped it on a letter lying on a desk. It immediately caught fire, sending flames shooting up the drapes to the ceiling.

Then the girls ecstatically ran to the room next door and set it alight too.

By the time a fire engine arrived at the burning store, Jennifer and June were outside, standing inconspicuously in the crowd of onlookers, watching the firemen in breathing apparatus rush into the blazing building.

"It was a picture that will live in my mind forever," wrote a joyous June in her diary that night. "It's been a long, painful, hard year. Don't I deserve to express my distress?"

The following morning when police arrived at Furzy Park to question them about the recent spate of fires, the twins played it cool. There was little evidence except the suspicions of neighbors, who had alerted police after seeing the smiling twins watching the blaze. When their questions were returned by the twins' blank stares, the officers left the house in frustration.

To the twins' delight, the fire made the front page of the local paper the following week. The article said that police were looking for a serial arsonist in the latest of a spate of fires that had already caused $150,000 in damage.

The twins now felt like big-time criminals, convinced it wouldn't be long before they found the fame and notoriety they so craved. To celebrate their success they decided to mark Guy Fawkes Night on November 5th in their own special way.

As millions of English families prepared to

set off fireworks and build bonfires, to com-
memorate Guy Fawkes' unsuccessful attempt to
burn down the Houses of Parliament in 1605,
the Gibbons girls went to work.

Breaking into a local school, they went on a
rampage of destruction, smashing furniture and
scrawling graffiti on the walls in felt-tip marker.
After stealing some clothes and books they set
a classroom on fire and fled.

Three days later a policeman spotted them
hurling a brick through a window of a local
technical college. As they broke in, the policeman summoned reinforcements, watching in
amazement as the two tiny figures inside began
lighting matches and dancing.

When police stormed the college, they were
just in time to stop Jennifer from dropping a
lighted match on the accelerant she'd already
sprayed around the room. Wrestling the waif-
like identical twins to the ground, they immediately arrested them, bringing down the curtain
on their lives of crime.

Seven months later June and Jennifer Gibbons
stood in the dock at Swansea Crown Court
accused of sixteen charges of theft and causing more than $250,000 in arson damage.
Dressed in matching blue anoraks, the ''Terrible Twins,'' as they had been branded by the
press, stared blankly into space muttering
''Guilty'' as each charge was read out. Aubrey
and Gloria Gibbons sat at the back of the court

in total disbelief that their nineteen-year-old daughters could possibly have committed such heinous crimes.

The tiny girls sat impassively in the dock as prosecutor John Diehl testified that June kept a diary, reveling in her crimes, and Jennifer had a love affair with arson.

A psychiatrist who had examined the twins after their arrest described them as psychopaths, who needed to be kept in maximum security, where they could be treated for their speech defects.

Sentencing the Gibbons twins to an indefinite stay at Broadmoor Hospital under the 1959 Mental Health Act, the judge, Mr. Justice Leonard, said he was satisfied that they were suffering from a "psychopathic disorder."

June and Jennifer showed no emotion as they were sent to England's most notorious hospital for the criminally insane for what amounted to a life sentence. The teenage twins became the youngest inmates at the maximum-security hospital, which contained some of Britain's worst murderers and serial killers.

On June 21, 1982—the longest day of the year—the Gibbons twins entered the imposing green gates of Broadmoor to start their sentence. Situated in the luscious green Berkshire countryside, sixty miles north of London, Broadmoor harked back to the Victorian Age and offered little inspiration to the adventurous twins.

Once inside they immediately retreated into a zombie-like state, refusing to eat with the other inmates in the dining hall. When Jennifer wouldn't leave her cell, the wardens showed no tolerance or understanding, physically dragging her to the bathroom. As usual June followed suit, refusing to acknowledge the staff or take part in any of the required activities.

At the end of their first week Jennifer attacked a female nurse and was placed in solitary confinement. Separated from the twin she loved and hated with equal intensity, June lapsed into a deep depression, attempting suicide by garroting herself with a belt. She too was then placed in solitary, where she staged a hunger strike, withdrawing into a catatonic state.

When Jennifer was let out of solitary and returned to the main hospital, she desperately pined for her sister. She would spend hours staring out the window hoping for a glimpse of June exercising in the garden below.

The twins' policy of non-cooperation became so disruptive that Broadmoor's chief medical officer, D. Boyce Le Couteur, decided to separate them permanently. But to provide an incentive for them to improve, doctors struck a deal, allowing them to meet on Saturday afternoons as a reward for being good.

As the months drew by, Jennifer and June

both became acclimated to the mind-numbing routine of Broadmoor. Every weekend their parents arrived for visits, bringing food and clothes. But the twins remained silent, letting the embarrassed Aubrey and Gloria do all the talking.

Although they refused to speak to doctors and staff, both girls' behavior slowly improved to the point where they were allowed to enjoy special privileges like social activities with Broadmoor's male patients.

Soon June and Jennifer both fell in love with a young inmate who had murdered his girlfriend. When he invited them to attend the hospital's Monday night disco, the girls were delighted, putting on their best dresses for the occasion. But their awkward shyness made communication impossible and the boy soon moved on to dance with another girl.

Before long Jennifer fell for another young murderer and determined, against all the odds, that she should have his baby. After the initial shock, the boy agreed and took one of Jennifer's cosmetic bottles to smuggle his sperm to her so she could later impregnate herself.

But Jennifer's hopes of having the first baby conceived and born inside Broadmoor collapsed when the authorities found out, banning the would-be parents from seeing each other.

As Jennifer dreamed of starting a family, her twin sister June became increasingly paranoid, convinced that the world was turning against her. Fearing that she was heading for a nervous breakdown, she steadfastly refused to conform to the rules, resisting renewed attempts to make her talk.

But the Broadmoor staff felt little pity for June after hearing her merrily chatting away to her twin every time they were allowed to see each other alone.

In a final attempt to break down the twins' resolve, doctors placed them both on regular injections of the tranquilizer Depixol. Usually prescribed to schizophrenics, the strong medication lessens aggression in disturbed patients, making them more compliant, but one of its side-effects is loss of concentration.

After taking the drug, Jennifer and June found they could no longer write creatively and they began losing their will to live. Jennifer developed frightening symptoms of schizophrenia, believing that the television was sending her strange messages. She became convinced that the KGB had put out a contract on her life and she would be shot in bed. As her hold on reality grew ever slimmer, her doses of medication were increased.

Over the next few years the drugs gradually achieved the desired effects, as the twins lost their spirit, resigning themselves to spending the rest of their lives in Broadmoor. They devoted themselves to romance, meeting a string of murderers and rapists at ward parties and discos and enjoying short-lived infatuations.

But inside both girls felt empty, resenting an uncaring world that had locked them away and thrown away the key.

"We are forgotten, faded away, never to be seen again," wrote June in her diary during her middle twenties.

Although they remained apart, Jennifer still refused to relinquish her hold on her twin sister, appearing to control her every movement like a wicked puppeteer.

Ironically, during their years in Broadmoor, Jennifer and June Gibbons achieved the fame they had once so craved when a biography about them, *The Silent Twins*, by English *Sunday Times* journalist Marjorie Wallace, was published in 1986. It resulted in a BBC television movie and was even turned into an avant-garde opera called *Jumelles*, which was performed in London in 1992.

As a reward for good behavior, June was allowed out of Broadmoor to attend the premiere at a London theater. While her story was played out on stage, using her poetry and short stories, June stood forlornly at the theater bar, looking on in glazed curiosity, under the careful guard of security staff from Broadmoor.

During their long years of incarceration, the Gibbons twins had watched Broadmoor undergoing a complete renovation to bring it into the twentieth century. As the world outside moved into the high-tech computer age, the Gibbons twins languished through the best years of their lives. They knew nothing of the new grunge music and Generation X, and remained locked in the past.

Exactly ten years after they had arrived at Broadmoor, doctors decided that the twins' condition had improved enough for them to be transferred to a less secure hospital. But after the initial excitement of hearing the good news came months of uncertainty, not knowing when they would be released or even if they would be reunited.

During their final weeks in Broadmoor the sisters became obsessed with death. Every morning they would meet before lessons and get into arguments about who would die first. Both girls had convinced themselves that one would now have to die in order for the other to survive. And in a chilling final chapter of their twinship, they entered a suicide pact which would finally set them free from each other.

In the early morning hours of June 9, 1993, June and Jennifer Gibbons were released from Broadmoor to travel to the newly built Caswell Clinic in Wales, where two places had been found for them near their family home. The previous day Jennifer had confided to June that she was feeling sick and couldn't eat or drink. She swore her twin to secrecy, saying that she didn't want the doctors to know in case they made her remain behind in Broadmoor for treatment.

Overnight, Jennifer's health deteriorated drastically but she stoically refused to seek medical help and her condition went unnoticed.

At the appointed hour of release the twins walked through the front gates of Broadmoor, carrying plastic bags containing the meager belongings they'd amassed during their twelve-year stay. Although Jennifer was unsteady on her feet, she managed the short distance to the minibus that would drive them the 140-mile journey to their new home in Bridgend, Wales.

As the van set off, Jennifer said that she felt tired and rested her head on June's shoulder.

"At last we're out of Broadmoor," she whispered before falling asleep.

A couple of hours later, when they pulled into a gas station, Jennifer could not be roused. The nurses seemed unconcerned, saying that it was probably the effects of the travel-sickness tablets she had taken before the journey.

By the time they arrived at the Caswell Clinic at 1 p.m. Jennifer had lost consciousness and had to be carried into the ward and put to bed. Doctors took her blood pressure and ordered tests, still maintaining that there was no cause for alarm.

But two hours later when June visited her sister she had the horrific realization that Jennifer had kept her part of their secret pact and was close to death. When the results of her blood test came through they revealed that Jennifer was perilously ill, suffering from acute hemolytic anemia, a drastic reduction of blood platelets.

Although Jennifer's eyes were open she was totally unresponsive and failed to recognize June or the doctors. She was rushed to the nearby Princess of Wales Hospital but within the hour she was dead.

Now that the psychic chains of bondage which had joined the twins from the womb had been broken, June Gibbons emerged a free woman and underwent a remarkable transformation. No longer under the mysterious control of her sister, she began to talk about her experience and come to terms with it.

"It was as if some kind of demon possessed her," June declared. "We were fighting for our souls. I am stronger than Jennifer and I have risen above it."

But like almost everything else in the twins' lives, Jennifer's death remained a mystery. A post mortem revealed that the twenty-nine-year-old had died from acute degeneration of the heart muscle, which rarely kills someone so young. At Jennifer's inquest a verdict of accidental death was recorded.

Although the doctors might have been surprised by her untimely death, June was not. She firmly believed that her twin sister had deliberately killed herself so that June could live for both of them.

In the months following Jennifer's death,

June made such good progress at the relaxed Caswell Institute that in March 1994 she was discharged back to her family. She was talking normally for the first time and had found a real boyfriend, without a criminal record. She now dreamed of marriage and settling down to raise her own family.

But although she changed her name to Allison in an effort to forget the past, the dead twin whom she loved and hated with such passionate intensity refused to go away.

"I feel guilty that I have survived and she hasn't," admitted June soon after her release. "Today I tell myself I'm just me. She became me and she would let me become her. We were the same person."

Seven

DOCTOR, DOCTOR

"But so much the more malign and wild does the ground become with bad seed and untilled"

—Dante Alighieri

William Terrell wiped the sweat from his brow as he entered the luxury Manhattan apartment building where he worked as a handyman. The phones were ringing off the hook again.

"It's just too damned hot," he griped under his breath as he crossed the lush green-carpeted lobby to the unmanned reception area. He was covering for Joe, the building's superintendent, who had gotten sick and left Terrell in charge. The phone hadn't stopped in two hours. It seemed as though everyone in the building had a problem and needed something repaired.

It was a dog day in mid-July and the heat wave that had gripped Manhattan for nearly a week showed no signs of breaking. His maintenance job at the luxury apartment building on Sutton Place was usually a breeze. He could spend weeks showing up for work and doing nothing more than reading newspapers and playing endless games of solitaire.

But the unrelenting mid-90s temperatures had taken their toll on the elegant building, with one air conditioner after another breaking down.

Over the telephone came the hysterical voice of an elderly resident on the tenth floor. "Bill, the smell's getting worse. There's definitely something wrong. I think it's a rat."

It was the latest in a stream of calls from the tenth floor over the last couple of days, complaining about a strange smell. At first Terrell had warded them off, saying that there was probably a dead rat in the incinerator. But the calls had kept coming.

Earlier that Thursday morning he'd even gone up to the tenth floor to investigate and had to admit there was a definite smell of something coming from apartment 10C.

Terrell knew the apartment belonged to that tramp of a doctor, Cyril Marcus, but he didn't want anything to do with it. Marcus might be a famous doctor but Terrell didn't consider him, or his twin brother, Stewart, who also called himself a doctor, the right sort of people for a respectable building like this. Doctors or no doctors, they had no manners, and dressed like bums.

Over the last few weeks he'd often seen one of the tall, skinny, dark-haired brothers shuffling past him through the lobby, carrying brown bags of groceries from Gristedes. But it was hard to tell them apart, as they were identical.

Even Joe had remarked last week that the doctors looked like Belsen camp victims. And although the temperatures were sweltering in the 90s they still wore long winter coats over their scrawny bodies and never said so much as a "Good-day."

"He may be rich but he looks more like a bag lady," Terrell had told Joe a few days earlier, as one of the doctors had shambled past reception and rushed into the elevator.

"I hear his identical twin moved in to 10C with him a couple of months ago and he's just as bad," Joe had replied. "They're two rotten peas in a pod."

Terrell was certain that the strange smell was probably nothing more than decaying food. But somebody must be there because he could hear music playing inside.

After knocking hard on the door three times without any response, the handyman shrugged his shoulders and gave up. He toyed with the idea of using the master key to gain access, but was distracted by another tenant, who demanded that he mend a leaking air conditioner immediately.

But Terrell had resigned himself to dealing with the smell in 10C, if only to get those damned tenth-floor residents off his back and get some peace.

"Okay, okay, I'll be up in a minute," said

Terrell, slamming down the phone in reception and grudgingly heading back to the elevator, jangling the set of master keys.

As he stepped out at the tenth floor several older tenants from neighboring apartments were already waiting for him.

"Rubberneckers," thought Terrell as he exited the elevator, trying to keep his temper.

Walking along the hall to 10C, Terrell had to admit the smell had gotten worse in the last few hours. He'd be damned if he'd ever smelled anything like it before. It certainly didn't smell like a dead rat. It was sort of sweet, come to think of it.

Opening the front door, he was almost knocked to the ground by the overpowering stench. He could almost see it. It seemed to have a presence of its own, like a dark, pungent gas.

Suddenly, in a blinding flash, he knew exactly what it was. And he wasn't being paid enough to deal with this.

Holding his nose he entered the hot apartment and saw a scene of filth and squalor almost beyond belief. The carpeted floor was completely buried under piles of dirty clothes, empty liquor bottles and rotting food. He felt sick as his heavy boots sank into the foot-deep garbage, the remains of scores of half-eaten TV dinners, empty soda cans and brown supermarket bags.

He grimaced, seeing hundreds of empty prescription bottles strewn around everywhere as he carefully negotiated his way through the narrow hall into the bedroom.

Terrell recoiled in horror as he entered and saw a shocking tableau in front of him. Dr. Cyril Marcus's rotting body was lying face down on the bed, dressed only in shorts. His twin brother Stewart's body was spread out on the floor less than three feet away, an outstretched arm desperately reaching out toward his brother, as if for help.

Before he could make it through the mounds of stinking garbage and out of the apartment, Terrell threw up as the other startled tenants looked on in astonishment.

When Anna Marcus gave birth to twins in 1930 she declared it a miracle. The arrival of a healthy set of identical twin boys caused quite a stir in the small town of Binghamton, New York. Her husband, Dr. Jack Marcus, a well-known general practitioner in the picturesque town, was also delighted. He couldn't wait to bring his new-born twin sons into his office to proudly show them off to his patients.

From their earliest days, Cyril Carlisle and Stewart Lee Marcus were always dressed alike and shared a double pram. Even their parents had difficulty telling them apart. Cyril, the eldest by two minutes, was the more introspective and serious of the two. Stewart was more boisterous and could be a real handful, and Anna was always telling him to be more like his well-behaved twin brother, who never caused trouble.

Although they grew up in the Depression, the Marcuses never suffered like their less-fortunate neighbors. Doctor Marcus's practice was flourishing but he took pride in treating his poorer patients for nothing or extending them generous credit. He had a strict code of medical ethics and tried to pass them on to his twin sons.

Anna Marcus kept an orthodox Jewish home and every Friday night the handsome, identically dressed twins would walk to synagogue with their father. After prayers they returned home with a huge appetite for one of Anna Marcus's Sabbath meals. It was a Marcus family tradition that the twin brothers adored.

As they grew up, their lives ran on the same parallel track. They attended the same infant school and by the time they reached public school they discovered that they could hoodwink their teachers by impersonating each other.

The Marcus twins shone at school. They were both excellent students and consistently at the top of their class. Although their teachers often suspected that Stewart was the smarter twin and did his brother's homework, the boys were never caught. During examinations Stewart would often impersonate Cyril and help him achieve the high grades that he never could have gotten on his own.

During childhood Stewart seemed to overshadow Cyril in everything. He had more self-confidence and was far more assertive than the quieter Cyril, who was happy to take a back seat.

When Dr. Marcus was offered a better practice in Bayonne, New Jersey, he moved his family south. To the twins it was a bitter disappointment. They loved running wild in the forests and open countryside of Binghamton and felt imprisoned in the drab industrial Bayonne.

From infancy, when their father first took them to his practice, the twins dreamed of becoming doctors. Fired by their father's passion for medicine, they believed it was their destiny. As children they would read medical text books together and dream of their future as famous doctors. Dr. Marcus, who had never quite realized his own medical ambitions to be a surgeon, was delighted by his sons' interest in the profession and encouraged them.

By their late teens, the Marcus twins were both six feet tall and, with their brooding good looks, had no trouble attracting girls. It wasn't long before Stewart had proved himself a ladies' man, proudly losing his virginity to the prettiest girl in their school. Not wanting his shyer brother to miss out on the experience, he encouraged Cyril to impersonate him on the next date and lose his too.

In years to come the twins would often double-date with willing girls, who enjoyed never quite knowing which twin they were in bed with. Sometimes, on single dates, the girls had no idea that they were even with a twin, and wondered why their lover's personality would subtly change each time they went out.

At eighteen years of age, the Marcuses were both accepted at Syracuse University and Medical School in upstate New York. Their father was delighted that they were following him into medicine and gave them generous allowances so they could dress like doctors and live comfortably.

Stewart and Cyril studied hard together, believing that they had more to prove as twins than their fellow students. They were both designated Phi Beta Kappa, impressing their professors, who saw them as prize students and singled them out for special attention.

By the end of their first year at Syracuse, the Marcus twins knew full well how gifted they were. There was nothing to stop them from getting to the very top of their chosen field of gynecology.

By the early 1950s the Marcus twins had graduated with high honors from Syracuse and seemed destined to achieve fame and fortune in the world of medicine. But their careers were put on hold when they were called up for Army service.

Doctors Cyril and Stewart Marcus had led identical lives. They had never been apart for a single day and had done everything together. With their all-American crew cuts and fastidious tastes in fashion, they created quite an impression at the Army hospital where they'd been assigned.

But within the vacuum of the twins' world there was a struggle for power. Cyril, always the weaker of the two, was depending more and more on Stewart to carry him through.

Photographs at the time reveal the inequality between the brothers. As Stewart brims with an almost arrogant self-confidence, Cyril looks vulnerable, with a haunted look in his eyes. Stewart's drive and ambition had brought them this far and Cyril had been content to ride on his coattails to success. But things would soon change drastically.

The Army quickly recognized the twins' excellence as doctors and promoted them to captains, appointing them joint chiefs of obstetrics and gynecology at their service hospital. And while some would have seen the Army as a waiting room for better things, the Marcuses used it to their advantage to launch themselves to the next stage of their medical careers.

When they were discharged from the Army

they both found positions in the obstetrics department at New York's prestigious Lenox Hill Hospital. But now the twins' relationship began to unravel.

Finally, at the age of twenty-eight, Cyril, longing for his own identity and career, began to assert his independence. Their paths finally split when Cyril was offered a residency at New York's Mount Sinai Hospital, under the tutelage of the renowned specialist Dr. Alan Guttmacher, and accepted it. The new job would give him the confidence he lacked and he would soon outpace his brother.

Furious that Cyril had cut the cord between them, Stewart accepted a residency at a hospital fifty miles away in Stanford, Connecticut. For the first time in their lives the Marcus twins found themselves separated and alone.

At Mount Sinai, Cyril began to shine for the first time without his brother's help. He developed a new confidence and began getting a reputation as *the* doctor to watch, the one who was going places.

In the late 1950s Manhattan was a swirl of parties and social events. As a handsome, single gynecologist, Dr. Cyril Marcus soon found himself much in demand by hostesses. Most evenings after finishing work he dashed home to prepare for an evening out on the town.

He became a fashion plate and spent most of his income on clothes, viewing it as a necessary way to be accepted by Manhattan society. He

bought a gleaming new Chevrolet and culti-
vated a rich, new persona, light years away
from his humble Binghamton roots, which he
carefully concealed.

Cyril began to portray himself as the scion
of a wealthy and successful Manhattan doctor.
With his excellent manners and scintillating
wit, he had no trouble maintaining his charade.

On weekends Stewart often drove into the
city to stay with him. The twins loved to
double-date, delighting in swapping identities
to sleep with each other's girlfriends, later re-
vealing their true identities to the girls, who often refused to believe they'd been fooled.
Afterward the twins took vicarious pleasure in
comparing notes.

But everything changed in 1960 when Cyril
fell in love with Corinne Stein, a beautiful
young Manhattan socialite. When they announced their engagement, Stewart was devastated that a woman had finally come between
him and his brother. Despite Stewart's pleas
that he stay single, Cyril married Corinne in a
lavish ceremony at a New York synagogue with
Stewart as best man.

A year earlier, Cornell Medical Center and
its affiliate New York Hospital had wooed Cyril
away from Mount Sinai with an offer too good
to refuse. He was appointed a clinical assistant
professor of obstetrics and gynecology and as
part of the deal, the hospital agreed to hire
Stewart in the same position.

Cornell Medical Center was a world-class hospital with a renowned obstetrics department. And now that the twins were reunited—at least professionally—it seemed as though nothing could stand in their way.

They took an office together on Manhattan's plush Upper East Side at 420 E. 72nd Street, and used Cyril's social connections to attract wealthy patients. Cyril loved mixing with Manhattan's rich and famous and within a year their practice was one of the hottest in New York, with a celebrity patient list that was the envy of their rivals.

"When you would take [their] calls it was like reading the Blue Book," recalled a nurse who used to work at their fashionable practice.

"They were scintillating personalities," said a woman who dated Stewart through the mid-1960s, and became close to both twins. "They were bright, good company, good-looking and very straight in their thinking and values."

Stewart often talked to her about his devotion to his mother and the sacrifices she had made to put the twins through medical school. But although the Marcus twins were social gadflies, they mainly kept to themselves at the hospital, making few friends among their medical colleagues.

As they did their daily hospital rounds, the handsome, identical twin doctors turned heads. Immaculately dressed in expensive clothes, they charmed their patients with wit and charisma.

But they were careful not to let their success go to their heads, making a point of attending professional meetings and closely questioning researchers presenting any new gynecological findings.

The Marcuses private practice was doing so well that the doctors rented two luxury apartments on fashionable Sutton Place, overlooking Manhattan's East River. Cyril and Corinne moved in on the tenth floor and Stewart moved into an apartment two floors above. It was the perfect location, just a few blocks away from Cornell Medical Center. And befitting their new positions as rich, successful young gynecologists they also bought a summer house in the Hamptons for weekends together.

The Marcuses career soared to even dizzier heights when they decided to specialize in discovering new breakthrough treatments for infertility. They began writing up their work for medical journals and soon caused a sensation in the world of gynecology.

In 1967, they became internationally recognized when they co-authored a book called *Advances in Obstetrics and Gynecology* which was published to great acclaim. It was hailed as ''brilliant'' by top gynecologist Dr. Gideon Panter, who described it as ''one of the major works'' in the field.

G. James Gallagher, who edited the twins'

book for the Baltimore publishing firm of Williams and Wilkins, remembers them driving a hard bargain over the contract and being utterly scrupulous over the final edit.

"They would take every word on every paragraph and go over it," said Gallagher.

The twins lovingly dedicated the book to their father, who had retired with their mother to Miami Beach. But the twins had little contact with their parents, telephoning only once or twice a year.

At just thirty-seven, the Marcus twins appeared to have the medical world at their feet. Their pioneering work in infertility seemed just the beginning of a glittering career that would leave its mark on the annals of medicine.

But already the almost mystical symbiosis they shared, which had been the key to their success, was beginning to turn against them.

When Nurse Barbara Jones started working at the twins' thriving practice in 1965, she didn't realize that Cyril, who had hired her, even had a twin brother. For the first week she marveled at how he could instantly travel between examining rooms like a superman. She even began to question whether she was seeing things as he kept appearing in one room after she'd just left him in another.

"He wasn't out of breath," she explained. "And his hands were scrubbed and his gloves were on already."

One day she was sitting at her reception desk when two identical Dr. Marcuses suddenly crossed paths right in front of her.

''And I yelled, 'Hold it!' But Cyril couldn't understand. He said, 'What is angering you? I told you that I had a brother.' ''

Eventually, Nurse Jones learned how to tell the twin doctors apart by Cyril's slightly higher voice and Stewart's better physique. But on several occasions she witnessed one of the twins starting a gynecological examination and the other completing it, with the patient remaining blissfully unaware that she'd been internally examined by two different doctors.

In 1968, Dr. Cyril Marcus's marriage began to disintegrate. He and Corinne now had two young daughters but his ever-increasing workload kept him away from the family for long periods of time. When Corinne asked for a divorce he was devastated.

After his divorce became final, Cyril fell into a deep depression and was inconsolable. On bad days he would stay in bed all day and refuse to see his patients, who would have to be treated by Stewart. Other days he would turn up at his practice and spend hours sitting on his office couch, listening to The Lettermen's hit ''Put Your Head on My Shoulder'' over and over again, to the annoyance of his staff.

''It really tore into him when they broke up,'' said Jones. ''He kept playing that record on the

PA in the office. It drove me crazy.''

Cyril longed for a reconciliation with Corinne and his children. He never admitted to friends and patients that his wife had left, continuing to discuss his family as if everything were fine.

Two years earlier Stewart had developed a back problem and began taking pain killers for relief. Now Cyril, desperately unhappy about his divorce, started writing himself prescriptions for pain killers to help him cope. He soon progressed to Dexedrine, an amphetamine which causes euphoria, and then began taking barbiturates to sleep at night.

The uppers and downers Cyril was taking often rendered him unfit to treat patients. So Stewart came to his rescue, impersonating him without patients having a clue that they were seeing a different doctor.

The increasing amounts of drugs Cyril was taking began to cause schizophrenic behavior. The once friendly, easy-going doctor would now become bad-tempered and hurl insults at the least provocation.

''He would sit down and you would see the expression on his face change,'' said Nurse Jones. ''And all of a sudden he would become a totally different person—arrogant, nasty, biting, cutting. I didn't think it was pills because he would snap back—you would see the facial expression—and then he would be back to himself.''

Nurse Jones finally resigned after Cyril threw a sterilizer full of instruments at her during a tirade. She walked out of the office and never returned.

Soon afterward Stewart began showing similar signs of instability. In 1969 he wrote to the twins' publishers to propose a follow-up to their successful book. He enclosed a list of possible contributors, saying that he had already spoken to many of them. The publisher liked the idea and signed a contract for a manuscript to be delivered in two years' time.

When the book failed to appear on the appointed date, the publisher tried calling the twins but never got a reply. Instead, he received a string of letters from angry doctors, complaining that the twins had never returned material they had provided for the new book.

The twin doctors' reputation was on the line in their close-knit medical circle. Many of their angry colleagues thought it ironic that Stewart had prefaced the first book by writing: "We will continue to be dependent upon the warm and gracious cooperation of our colleagues."

By the early 1970s, the twin were desperately trying to maintain their practice through a chemical haze. Cyril was addicted to barbiturates and his brother was also using them, to a lesser extent. They regularly made vital medical decisions and performed intricate gynecological surgery while under the influence of drugs.

Hospital colleagues and patients began to wonder what was wrong with Cyril, who had little attention span and seemed constantly distracted. The once-fastidious doctor hardly bothered with his appearance and had lost so much weight that his clothes hung off his tall, fragile body. But whenever questions were asked, Stewart would always make excuses for him refusing to acknowledge that anything was amiss.

In the summer of 1972, Cyril Marcus took an overdose of barbiturates. When he failed to arrive at his practice for an important meeting, his brother and a friend broke into his Sutton Place apartment, where they found him unconscious. When a concerned neighbor saw them breaking in and asked what was happening, Stewart angrily turned around and shouted, "Fuck off! My brother is ill."

Although many of their colleagues at New York Hospital began to suspect that the increasingly erratic twins had a problem, no one dared confront them about it, as they were still held in such high regard. Besides, there was an unwritten code among doctors to always protect each other.

On one occasion Cyril, obviously under the influence of drugs—he was sweating profusely and unsteady on his feet—walked into the operating theater to perform surgery. During the complicated operation he suddenly went berserk, ripping the anesthetic mask from his patient's face and placing it over his own.

When alarmed nurses finally persuaded him to let another doctor take over the operation, Stewart walked in to continue. But he too seemed as out of it as his twin brother.

Things came to a head at the hospital when Cyril Marcus completely messed up an operation. He was ordered to take a three-month leave of absence and seek psychological counseling from New York Hospital, but before long he was allowed to return to his medical duties under the watchful eyes of his colleagues.

The Marcus twins' decline was also apparent in their total disregard for all medical paperwork. They failed to fill out patient insurance forms and refused to forward medical records to other doctors when requested.

When the board of censors of the Medical Society of the County of New York started receiving a stream of complaints about Dr. Cyril Marcus, they ordered him to appear before a hearing to explain himself.

After canceling several scheduled appearances, Cyril finally met with board chairman Dr. Roger Steinhardt. At the interview he was totally unapologetic. Declaring that he would rectify the matter, he stormed out of the hearing.

"His behavior through this whole thing was so unexpected," said Dr. Steinhardt. "We began to wonder whether we were dealing with an errant physician or a sick physician."

The board then summoned Stewart to a hearing to ask if his twin was under strain and needed help. Stewart was furious at the allegation and angrily denied that there was anything wrong. He too walked out, refusing to have anything further to do with the board.

Over the next two years the Marcuses let their practice slide even further. It was as if they no longer cared what happened to it. Patients noticed that their once-spotless office had become filthy and was never cleaned. A refrigerator was stuffed with urine specimens that had never been sent for analysis. Many patients were so horrified by the decline that they changed doctors.

The twin gynecologists now rarely bothered to attend New York Hospital for appointments and surgery. Weeks passed with neither brother making an appearance. And when they did show the results were often disastrous.

On March 6, 1974, Nurse Kathy Rowland was assigned to assist Dr. Cyril Marcus in a simple circumcision. The pretty young nurse had six years' experience at New York Hospital but nothing had prepared her for working with Cyril.

She entered the operating room to find the distinguished gynecologist already scrubbed up and dressed for surgery. But as he started to perform the operation she grew increasingly horrified at his condition.

"I noticed he was sweating profusely,"

Nurse Rowland would later testify at a New York State medical inquiry. "He was a little unsteady on his feet and his hands were shaking."

Nurse Rowland was so concerned that she left the operating theater to tell her head nurse that Dr. Marcus looked ill. She was then instructed to return to the operation and look after the doctor.

"I asked him if he felt all right," recalled the nurse. "And he got quite mad at me and said, 'Stop asking me all those questions.'

"He was like off-balance and he kind of just separated his feet a little bit to keep his balance. I was very frightened for the baby. He could have cut off the whole penis for all I know."

Nurse Rowland was even more horrified when Dr. Marcus clamped the baby's penis and began trying to cut the foreskin using the blunt handle of a bladeless knife.

"I said, 'What are you doing?' And he turned and looked at me and said, 'I know I don't have the blade on,' and he put it on."

Dr. Cyril Marcus then went on to complete the operation. Afterward the frightened nurse never dared file a report on the incident, as she didn't think anyone would believe her. A year later, Stewart Marcus too had to abandon a circumcision when he was not sober enough to perform surgery.

By the beginning of 1975, it was an open secret at New York Hospital that the Marcus twins were no longer in full possession of their faculties and posed a dangerous medical hazard. They had virtually ceased to function as doctors, spending most of their time behind locked doors at Cyril's tenth-floor Sutton Place apartment, getting stoned on barbiturates.

They would often stay in the flat for days, eating corned beef sandwiches and TV dinners and drinking bottles of soda that Stewart collected from the nearby Gristedes supermarket.

In the six months prior to March 1975, the Marcuses admitted just eighteen patients into New York Hospital, compared with the several hundred that would have been expected. Then the twins stopped making admissions altogether.

In April, one of Cyril's long-time private patients, Susan Wright, who was expecting her second child, arrived for her monthly check-up to find a handwritten sign on the door, reading, "Come back on Tuesday at the same time."

Wright returned on Tuesday to find the Marcuses nurse waiting outside the office, having been locked out. The nurse said that the doctors had disappeared and she was tired of covering up for them. All she wanted was to resign and get the wages she was owed.

"I think it's the drugs," she told Wright. "I think you should get another doctor."

When Wright began asking whether Corinne Marcus realized that her husband had a drug problem, the nurse informed her that the couple had divorced years earlier.

"That was a complete shock," said Wright, an actress who had become close friends with Cyril Marcus over the eleven years that he had been her gynecologist, "because the entire time I'd gone to him he'd talked as though everything was fine with him and his wife."

A few weeks later Dr. Fritz Fuchs, New York Hospital's chief of obstetrics and gynecology, summoned the forty-five-year-old twin doctors into his office. He told them that they wouldn't be reappointed to their positions in the hospital when their contracts ran out at the end of June. He cited their strange behavior and medical problems as the reason.

Although Dr. Fuchs was deeply affected by the decision to terminate two once-brilliant careers, the Marcus twins took the news calmly and even looked relieved.

Feeling sorry for them, he agreed to give them a second chance and reconsider their cases if they took medical leaves to sort themselves out, but the twins both refused.

On June 17th, Dr. Stewart Marcus was summoned to New York Hospital for a medical emergency after his patient Gwyneth Williams suffered a miscarriage at four months and started to hemorrhage. Gwyneth, the wife of well-known New York Channel 7 television anchorman Eddie B. Williams, had called Stewart in agony and he'd agreed to meet her at New York Hospital within the hour.

By the time Stewart finally arrived in the emergency room three hours later, he could hardly stand up. He was so disoriented during his examination that he almost fell on top of Mrs. Williams several times. And as Eddie Williams watched in horror, Dr. Marcus began wiping his wife's blood onto his suit from his hands.

Although she was still bleeding profusely, Dr. Marcus suddenly asked Mrs. Williams whether she felt well enough to go home. He then began complimenting Eddie Williams on the shoes he was wearing, totally forgetting that he was in the middle of an emergency operation.

Fearing for his sick wife, Williams marched Stewart straight out of the operating room, telling him not to dare touch his wife in his present condition. Genuinely surprised, Dr. Marcus asked, ''What condition?''

Then Williams told him to go home and sleep it off and, after personally escorting him off the premises, arranged for another doctor to complete the operation. It would take Gwyneth Williams more than a year to recover psychologically from her ordeal with Dr. Stewart Marcus.

On July 1, 1975, their contract with Cornell Medical Center ran out and the Marcus twins found themselves on their own. They lost all hospital privileges and were virtually outlawed by the medical establishment.

Retreating to Cyril's apartment at Sutton Place, the twins started writing themselves larger and larger prescriptions for barbiturates and Dexedrine to satisfy their cravings for drugs.

By now Cyril Marcus had given up dressing and washing altogether, spending his days and nights getting high and watching television. Every couple of days his brother would throw on some clothes and walk the two blocks to First Avenue to buy TV dinners, cans of beans and sodas from Gristedes. He would then buy a couple of bottles of liquor before returning to Sutton Place.

The once-fastidious Cyril, who used to hate seeing a dirty Kleenex in his office wastepaper basket, now wallowed in his own filth and didn't care. The six-footer had lost so much weight that he looked like a walking skeleton as he drifted in and out of his warped barbiturate reality.

The formerly elegant apartment had become a garbage dump overflowing with the half-eaten dinners and empty soda bottles which were piled up on the floor.

Stewart was in a slightly better condition than his twin brother, as he hadn't been addicted as long. He was now doing the thinking for both of them.

Realizing the depths they had sunk to, he persuaded Cyril that they should make a final, valiant effort to clean up from drugs by going cold turkey. After they kicked dope, he said, they would triumphantly attend a New York Hospital medical board meeting on July 10th, where they had been given one final chance to rehabilitate themselves and get their old jobs back. Perhaps, he told Cyril, the Marcus twins could restore their reputations and soar to new heights in the medical world.

But as a doctor, Stewart fully realized the dangers of withdrawal from long-term addiction to heavy doses of barbiturates, a drug harder to kick than heroin. Sudden withdrawal can cause convulsions, delirium and even death from the collapse of the heart and circulatory system.

It seemed fitting that the Marcus twins should start their cold turkey on Independence Day. That morning Stewart collected all the remaining prescription bottles littering the apartment and threw their contents down the incinerator so they wouldn't be tempted to change their minds.

Then he ventured out of the tenth-floor apartment onto First Avenue for the last time to buy the supplies they would need to survive. It was a Friday and the start of a long holiday weekend and Stewart knew it was the perfect time to quit as the building would be virtually empty.

New York was sweltering in a heat wave and the airless city streets hit him like a blanket.

There had been no garbage collection and the gaseous smells rising up from the concrete were almost overpowering.

When he shambled into Gristedes Supermarket on 62nd Street the few customers inside turned around in disgust, thinking that the tall, thin, unkempt-looking man in the thick overcoat was a tramp. The manager had grown used to the eccentric doctor over the last few weeks. Today he looked even worse than usual, but the grocer knew better than to ask prying questions.

After pulling out a bundle of one-dollar bills from his coat pocket to pay, Dr. Stewart Marcus returned to the apartment, carrying two brown bags overflowing with junk food and soda. He was glad that the super, Joe, wasn't sitting in the reception area to register his disapproval.

Back in the apartment, Stewart double-locked the front door and walked through the piles of rubbish to the bedroom, where his twin brother was lying incoherent on the bed. The smell inside seemed to have gotten worse in the thirty minutes since he had left. The air conditioner had long given up working and it was even hotter inside than out.

"It's Independence Day. Let's celebrate by kicking this devil once and for all," said Stewart, as he opened a fast-melting iced cake with an American flag on top.

Dr. Stewart Marcus was the first to die. He was hit by convulsions from the withdrawal as he lay naked on the bed. When Cyril realized that his twin had finally left him, he too lost the heart to survive. Using every ounce of his remaining strength, he dragged his twin's body onto the floor, lay down on the bed and waited to join him.

Eight

TIM-TODD

"Body and spirit are twins: God only knows
which is which"

—*The Higher Pantheism in a Nutshell* [1880]

On a cool December evening, Temple City Deputy Sheriffs Jim McDivett and Steve Race were called to an apartment building to investigate a shooting. The call had come in a few minutes earlier to radio dispatchers at the sub–police station on the outskirts of Los Angeles, from a hysterical woman requesting an ambulance.

As the officers drew up at the plush two-story apartment building at 5324 Baldwin Avenue, a distraught young man, wearing a striped monogrammed shirt, burst out of the manager's office. He introduced himself as Tim and led the officers through an office and into a courtyard, ushering them into the owner's apartment. Once inside he stopped and pointed toward the bedroom. He then withdrew into the kitchen, poured himself a large vodka and started to cry.

McDivett and Race slowly entered the bedroom with their guns drawn but were unprepared for the strange sight awaiting them. Lying on the bed was Tim's exact double; the only difference was he was dying. Wearing the same monogrammed shirt as his clone in the kitchen, the fatally wounded Todd Nicholson had been shot through the heart. A bloodstained towel lay under his head and blood was oozing from his mouth. On the floor by the bed lay a recently fired bolt-action .22 caliber Winchester rifle.

After telling his partner to check on the ambulance, McDivett noted the lavishly decorated room with its modern art, rare antiques and custom-built television console. "These are rich kids," thought McDivitt, wondering if he had walked into a real-life episode of Rod Serling's *Twilight Zone*.

Later he would discover that, although Tim was only twenty-two, he owned the entire building and was a successful multimillionaire businessman. As they waited for the ambulance to arrive, McDivett questioned Tim in the kitchen about what had happened that night. Although it seemed obvious, he first asked the dead man's identity.

"He's my brother," stuttered Tim, choking back the tears. "My twin brother. I shot him. I shot him."

Timothy Wills and Todd Fenlon Nicholson were born in Tulsa, Oklahoma, on August 2, 1942, into a world of riches and privilege, descended from three powerful Chicago family dynasties. Todd was the first-born by two minutes but it was a gap that would tragically define the twins' lives.

Their father, Edward Carry Nicholson, had grown up in Chicago, the spoiled son of the fabulously wealthy Pullman family, who had made their fortune as meatpackers and industrialists. As a young boy he sat on his grandfather's lap at Pullman Company board meetings, lighting the magnate's cigars to the amusement of the other board members. Then his proud grandfather would tip him a five-dollar bill.

Growing up, Edward lived the life of a playboy, with a passion for beautiful women, hard drink and guns. It would be a trait his twin sons would inherit. By his early twenties Ted, as he was called, was one of the most eligible bachelors in Chicago and could pick and choose from the young society ladies.

But his head was turned by a twenty-five-year-old farmer's daughter from upstate Michigan named Roberta Wills. He loved her fierce independence, finding her unpretentious working-class roots a welcome change from the prim and proper debutantes he usually dated.

The couple married in 1940 and their wedding picture made all the Chicago society columns. But a year later America entered World War II and Ted moved his young wife to Tulsa, Oklahoma, becoming a civilian glider instructor for the U.S. Air Force.

The newly married couple had little in common. While Ted was well-educated and sophisticated, Roberta was considered common by many of his friends and she often embarrassed him in public with her coarse swearing.

By the time Tim and Todd were born he was ready to move on, declaring that twins gave him the creeps. He decided to become a movie producer, and relocated the family to Hollywood. Roberta and the twins moved into a hillside home, while Ted took up residence in a swanky bachelor apartment to pursue what he called ''the bottle and broads.''

At the end of the war the couple divorced and Roberta was left to bring up the twins as a single mother on a monthly trust fund check. She was devastated and blamed her twin sons for the loss of her husband; she would never forgive them.

As Tim and Todd Nicholson grew up even Roberta couldn't tell them apart. The only difference between them was that Tim was left-handed and Todd was right-handed. To solve the problem Roberta began calling them ''Tim-Todd,'' regardless of which one she was talking to. She dressed them identically and treated them as one person, with the result that even the twins wondered where one finished and the other began.

From their earliest days, the Nicholson twins desperately tried to break free and assert their individuality. Although totally dependent on each other they soon developed a bitter rivalry that would have disastrous effects.

"Todd was the first to be born," Tim Nicholson would later explain. "I came along two minutes later. Those two minutes made a difference."

Sleeping in identical cots, Tim and Todd would fall asleep gripping each other's hands so tightly that Roberta could hardly pry them apart in the morning. Awake, they would compete for their mother's attention as she cursed and slapped them into obedience. But it wasn't long before she gave up trying to control them and let them run wild.

When the two cherubic-faced twins started school in La Jolla, California, they were impossible to tell apart. Their teachers, frustrated by their constant fighting and wild behavior, split them up in different classrooms. But Tim and Todd always had the last laugh by impersonating each other to fool their teachers. It was a thrilling game for the twins, one that they would later employ successfully with girls.

The school authorities eventually expelled the Nicholson twins, declaring them out of control. Roberta's neighbors were also turning up at their house, complaining about the twins' bad influence on their children. Before long Tim and Todd found themselves outcasts in their community.

Roberta tried to knock some discipline into her wild seven-year-old sons, enrolling them in military school, but their behavior became even worse. Their rebelliousness was well-admired by their fellow cadets, though, who gave them the joint nickname "TNT."

Every weekend the twin cadets were punished, spending hours marching around the parade-ground flagpole. Like identical toy soldiers, Tim and Todd would proudly hold their tiny toy rifles over their shoulders during the punishment sessions. Their only regret was that they only had toys. When they complained to their instructors, they were given real rifles but were too weak to carry them.

A few months later their lives changed forever when their father suddenly reappeared. He persuaded Roberta to let him take the twins to his home in Costa Rica to live with his new girlfriend. As they settled in Costa Rica, their playboy father found it impossible to tell them apart. He finally solved the problem by embroidering their names on their shirts.

With their own private tutor, baby-sitter and chauffeur, Tim and Todd loved their new life and the freedom that came with it. The neighboring Costa Rican farmers treated them like "little gods," believing that twins brought good luck and rich harvests.

They spent their days reading comics, going to movies and taking turns peeping through the bedroom keyhole of their beautiful German tutor to watch her undress. It became yet another game for the twins to assert their one-upmanship over each other.

One day Ted Nicholson decided that his eight-year-old sons should learn to drink. While they were out driving he brought out a quart bottle of gin from the glove compartment and told them to taste it.

"I figured it was his way of teaching us to be men," remembered Tim. "Wanting him to know that I was a good pupil I took a big swallow of the stuff. It was like someone had got a stranglehold of my throat, and fire was raging all the way down to my gut."

As the little boy doubled up in pain, his father snatched the bottle away and handed it to Todd, leaving Tim feeling like a failure.

A few months later their mother arrived in Costa Rica for a family reunion. But the reconciliation was short-lived due to Ted Nicholson's heavy drinking and constant womanizing.

One day after a major row Ted walked out on his family a second time. Roberta remained in Costa Rica for a few months with her new boyfriend, Ramon, but then returned to California with the twins, sending them back to their old military school.

Tim and Todd were furious with their mother for making them give up their freedom in Costa Rica. They hated returning to military school with its ultrastrict discipline, and were no longer popular with the other cadets, who made cruel jokes about them. So the twins withdrew into each other, deciding to become outlaws.

One day at the beach an older boy began mocking Todd and a fight ensued. Tim came to his rescue, throwing sand in the boy's face. Then he grabbed a broken bottle and attacked him, slashing his thigh with the razor-sharp glass.

The police were summoned as the twins made their escape. A few hours later an officer arrived at their house to investigate. When he asked who had stabbed the boy, Tim and Todd both owned up, leaving the bewildered officer helpless to make an arrest without knowing the true culprit.

It was the first time Tim and Todd had been put to the test. They now believed themselves invulnerable—if they stuck together.

"It was us against the world," Tim would later say.

As the Nicholson twins grew into adolescence, their always-troubled relationship with their mother turned violent. Roberta was drinking heavily and had little patience for her rebellious sons. In the summer of 1951 she decided to rent a cottage in Maine to be near her younger sister. Loading all their possessions into her Cadillac convertible, mother and sons set off cross-country with a .22 Belgium automatic under the seat for protection.

Tim and Todd fought constantly on the journey and Roberta kept stopping to slap them into compliance. At one point she got so angry that she threw them out of the car, saying she wanted to be rid of them. Then she drove off, abandoning them by the roadside in tears. A few minutes later she relented, returning to pick them up again. They continued the journey as if nothing had happened.

At their new school in Boothbay, Maine, the Nicholson twins bitterly clashed with other pupils who saw them as freaks. Before long they were on the move again, this time to Washington, D.C.

Roberta loved the social whirl of Washington and began going to parties every night. She sent for Ramon, installing him into her new home and having as little to do with her twin sons as possible.

Tim and Todd were left alone in the basement of the house for hours at a time. Their only distraction was to smash furniture and play marathon games of Monopoly, which they adored. They would pretend to be real-estate moguls, experiencing the exhilaration of power for the first time. The game whetted their appetites for business competition with each other, helping to develop a rivalry between them that would later be their downfall.

In 1953 they turned eleven, and Roberta ordered twin birthday cakes, inviting her new Washington friends to their birthday party. Unfortunately she refused to allow Tim and Todd to attend, leaving them outside the front room helplessly staring at their birthday cakes.

Eventually they couldn't stand it any longer and burst into the party to cut their cakes. Roberta was furious.

"That cake's for decoration only," she snapped, ordering them back to their bedroom, "and you little bastards aren't getting any of it until I'm good and ready."

The twins blamed each other for being barred from their own birthday party. Tim became so angry that he went upstairs and destroyed the telescope he'd just given Todd as a birthday present.

Before long, the ever-restless Roberta had tired of Washington. She moved the boys south to Fort Lauderdale, Florida, for the winter and sent Ramon back to Costa Rica. In her late thirties and fast losing her beauty, Roberta started drinking to escape the sad reality of her life.

"I remember her coming in from the marina one night and finding Todd and me in the midst of a knock-down-drag-out brawl," said Tim. "She was pretty juiced up and decided she'd had it with us. She ran into the bedroom screaming, 'You dirty little sons of bitches, I can't stand it any longer. I want you out of my life. I'm going to kill you.' "

Then she picked up her automatic and started chasing Tim and Todd, who ran for their lives.

As teenagers the twins discovered girls and opened up an exciting new area of competition.

Most nights they would go to stag films and roll home in the early hours to find their mother drunk and often incoherent. They soon fixed their sights on seeing who could lose his virginity first. When Tim finally bedded an older student on a building site, he rushed home in triumph to tell Todd.

On hearing the news Todd went berserk, attacking his twin with a heavy lawn sprinkler. When Roberta heard the commotion she smashed a heavy china mug over Todd's head, stopping him in his tracks. It would take Todd another two years to catch up sexually with his twin brother and square things between them.

Before long Roberta had tired of Florida and took the boys back to California to be near their millionaire grandfather, Colonel Nicholson, who lived in Santa Barbara. They moved into a house near him and Tim and Todd found jobs as paper boys to earn extra pocket money. But their competitive spirits soon led to fights at the pick-up point, where they vied to be first to collect the papers.

''We'd fight until we'd figured we'd equalized the amount of pain we'd inflicted on the other,'' recalls Tim. ''And then the fight would stop as suddenly as it began, and we'd share the candy bar one of us might happen to have in his pocket.''

While Tim occupied himself with girls, Todd found a job in a garage to learn about cars. By their sixteenth birthdays, they had saved enough money to buy a '53 Ford V8, causing quite a stir among their school friends, who nicknamed them "the twins with the fast car."

One day Tim urged Todd to impersonate him and lose his virginity with one of his girlfriends. Todd was only too happy to oblige and afterward told the girl his true identity. But she absolutely refused to believe he wasn't Tim.

In 1960 Ted Nicholson died of liver failure at the age of forty-one, leaving his twin sons half a million dollars each in a trust fund. They would receive the money on their twenty-first birthday, or before if they married.

Roberta was furious that her ex-husband hadn't left her a cent and unsuccessfully sued to become guardian of her sons' estate. Although Tim and Todd were to receive a monthly allowance of $400, they insisted on retaining their independence by working part-time. They had soon saved up enough money to buy identical matching Starliner convertibles.

Now that they were rich they decided to drop out of high school without graduating to make their own way in the world. Todd joined the Naval Reserve; Tim tried to outdo him by joining the Marines, but was discharged after a fight which injured his back.

After leaving the Marines, Tim moved into a small apartment with his twin brother in Santa Monica. It was there that their bitter rivalry in women and business turned violent.

One day Todd told Tim that he was having an affair with a recently divorced nurse named Patricia, who had two young children. Singing her sexual praises, Todd invited his twin to impersonate him and try her out.

When Tim approached her for the first time on a beach, Patricia thought he was Todd and chastised him for his Marine buzz cut. Before long Tim had seduced her and his sexual technique made her realize that she was not sleeping with Todd. When Patricia decided she preferred Tim, Todd rebounded by finding himself another willing divorcée named Sherry.

Things turned ugly when Tim threatened the twins' sacred bond and announced that he was planning to marry Patricia. Todd flew into a fury and claimed Patricia was still sleeping with him behind Tim's back. Tim accused his brother of lying even though he suspected it might be true. Then he defiantly married Patricia anyway to spite Todd.

Soon after their marriage Tim confronted Patricia about cheating on him with Todd. After initially denying it, she came clean and admitted it, saying that it was like sleeping with the same person.

Tim then had the marriage annulled on the grounds that he was only twenty and had lied about his age on the marriage certificate. But he urged the now-pregnant Patricia to stay with him, promising to marry her when he was twenty-one. When she gave birth to a son, Tim was never certain whether he or Todd was the true father.

After their break-up Patricia would accuse Tim of savagely beating her throughout the relationship.

"He left me with black and blue marks and once deafened me with a blow to the ear," she would recall.

Soon after Tim's marriage, Todd married his divorcée girlfriend Sherry to free up his share of the trust fund. That marriage was also annulled after Todd accused Sherry of marrying him for money.

The twins' broken marriages just represented the latest round in the fast-escalating battle between them for one-upmanship.

"We couldn't stay apart," said Tim. "We always had to be watching each other, then try stopping what the other was up to if we didn't care for it."

It was a high-stakes game that would eventually end in death.

In the summer of 1963 the Nicholson twins turned twenty-one and decided to become businessmen, taking night classes in financial administration. Having now come of age they claimed their $1 million inheritance and moved fast.

In separate business deals, Tim bought a large apartment building in Temple City, in the sprawling suburbs of Los Angeles, while his twin brother looked to Phoenix, Arizona, where he purchased a new office building. Todd then rented out apartments to prostitutes, buying a 7.5 Mauser automatic to protect himself against pimps who might feel threatened by him moving into their territory.

A few months later Todd telephoned Tim with an exciting new business opportunity. He offered his twin brother a partnership in a scheme to manufacture inflatable party dolls, to be sold via mail order.

Todd enthusiastically told Tim that the five-foot five-inch voluptuous blonde bikinied doll would make them millions of dollars. But Tim, who had recently bought his own private plane, decided instead to invest in a gold mine in Nicaragua and flew out to supervise operations.

On his flight back to America, Tim struck up a conversation with a fellow passenger named Anita Day. When they landed in Los Angeles he invited the twenty-two-year-old blonde model back to his Baldwin Arms apartment where they became lovers.

A few days later Todd telephoned asking for help, as he had run into problems with his party-doll business. Tim flew out to Phoenix with Anita, arriving late at night to find that Todd was not at home. Tim finally persuaded the super to let him into the apartment by pretending to be his brother. Then he told Anita to go to sleep in Todd's king-sized bed while he waited for Todd.

When Todd arrived he was delighted to see Tim after so many months apart. But his mood changed when he walked into his bedroom and discovered Anita asleep naked in his bed. Flying into a ''psychotic rage,'' Todd threatened to kill his twin brother.

''He came with his Mauser automatic in hand screaming that he was going to kill me,'' Tim later recalled. ''All I could think of was where the bullet was going to hit and how it was going to feel. It was only later that I learned he'd actually pulled the trigger but the gun had jammed.''

As Anita quickly dressed, Todd pistol-whipped Tim, throwing him out of the apartment to spend the night in a motel nursing his injuries. The next morning the twins held a business meeting, totally ignoring the previous night's violence.

Todd's business schemes never seemed to pan out. His sex doll was too expensive to produce profitably and his Phoenix office building began losing money. To make things even worse, Tim's business ventures succeeded and Todd became depressed, bitterly resenting his brother's success.

Todd looked for distractions and became engaged to Rita Musgrave, a Phoenix divorcée and mother of two. Rita saw first-hand the intense antagonism between the twins which could explode into violence at any time.

"They could flare up over anything," she would later explain. "But they loved each other."

Todd's increasing unpredictable volatility was fast becoming a threat to everyone around him. On one occasion he beat up his own mother so badly that her face had to be surgically rebuilt.

"He struck me in the face," Roberta would later testify. "He knocked my teeth loose and I had two black eyes. My jaw was dislocated and my nose and mouth were bloodied."

Deciding that Todd would be happier in Los Angeles, Tim persuaded him to sell his business interests in Phoenix and move in with him. Todd agreed to exchange his $300,000 Phoenix property as part payment for a $1.3 million West Hollywood apartment house.

"They were real nice boys," said Los Angeles Realtor Harold Ivers, who negotiated the sale. "They worked as a team and got along famously. They showed a lot of love and affection for one another."

On Monday, December 7, 1964, Tim rose early, showered and put on his best business suit. He was flying himself to San Diego for a business meeting to obtain financing for a new project. Additionally, he would meet his mother, who was now living outside San Diego, for lunch. Todd agreed to drive Tim to the airfield, where his single-engine airplane was hangared, saying he was to busy to go along on the trip.

At lunch, Roberta told Tim that Todd had secretly taken out a million-dollar life insurance policy on Tim's life, impersonating him in the required physical examination. She expressed fears that Todd planned to murder him during an upcoming trip to Nicaragua. Refusing to believe Todd was capable of it, Tim called her stupid and changed the subject.

At the end of the four-hour lunch, Roberta drove Tim to the airport and he flew his plane back to Los Angeles.

It was already dark when Tim arrived back at the Baldwin Arms and sought out his brother. Seeing that the lights were on in the apartment where Todd was staying, Tim went in to discover one of his employees, Ernest Bernal, making a long-distance call to his wife in Phoenix. Tim was furious at being taken advantage of and ordered him to hang up, threatening to fire him.

Tim then walked over to his apartment to find Todd taking a shower. He returned a few minutes later as Todd was dressing for a night on the town. When Todd announced that he planned to return to Phoenix and start again, Tim was furious, fearing that his unpredictable twin would jeopardize the deal he'd just secured.

Tim would later testify: "I said to Todd, 'I want to get one thing straightened out. We've got a building in escrow. You're out of Phoenix now. I don't want a duplicate of what happened in Phoenix. You're not going to have the attitude you had there.' ''

Todd's eyes glazed over and his face contorted in rage as the cologne bottle he had been holding fell to the floor and smashed.

"You son of a bitch," screamed Todd. "You're not going to talk to me like that. I'll kill you."

Fearing that Todd was going for his pistol as he had done in the past, Tim ran into the bedroom to fetch his rifle from a gun rack on the wall. Todd stormed into the bedroom behind him.

"I turned around," a tearful Tim would later recall, "and I said, 'You're not going to grab that gun. I'll kill you!' ''

Tim fired the rifle at his brother but missed, the bullet ripping through the bed and into the floor. Todd stood there stunned that his younger twin had actually fired the rifle.

Tim loaded another shell into the chamber and aimed it at Todd, point-blank. He pulled the trigger again, this time dispatching the bullet straight into Todd's heart. As his twin brother fell to the floor dying, he looked at Tim with blank astonishment.

Tim would be haunted by that look for the rest of his life. He would see it as his twin brother's final admission of defeat combined with admiration.

"You did it! You actually shot me," Todd

appeared to be saying as his lifeblood poured out of him.

When detectives told Tim that his twin brother was dead he fell apart. He dropped to the floor weeping hysterically and repeatedly calling out his brother's name. His anguished cries tore through his apartment building, bringing the other tenants out to investigate.

A little after 11 that night, Tim was arrested for murder and taken to the Temple City police station, where he was placed in a cell. For the first time in his life he was alone, having finally broken free of his twin brother. But he still looked to Todd for reassurance, carrying on a dialogue with his dead twin throughout the night.

The next morning the story exploded in front-page headlines across America. It had all the sensational ingredients: rich playboy twins, murder, lust and greed.

RICH TWIN SLAIN; BROTHER HELD, trumpeted the *Los Angeles Times*, RICH HEIR HELD IN KILLING OF TWIN, announced the *San Francisco Chronicle*, and the normally reserved *New York Times* even carried the story under the headline, PULLMAN HEIR HELD IN DEATH OF TWIN BROTHER.

Two days after the killing, Tim was arraigned and charged with murdering his twin brother Todd. The bizarre story of the Nicholson twins' murderous relationship had all the hallmarks of Greek tragedy. It was an epic tale of murder, sex and self-destruction.

Tim Nicholson's murder trial opened at the Pasadena Supreme Court on May 3, and captured the imagination of the American public. In the absence of any clear-cut motive the trial turned into a public dissection of the strange, almost mystical twin relationship.

In day after day of riveting testimony, the court heard how the twins had struggled for their own identity since birth. Each of their desperate attempts to break free from each other had been thwarted. It was as if nature had played a cruel joke, trapping one being in two bodies with death as the only way out.

"This is a unique case, Tim and Todd," Tim would try and explain in 1998. "We always competed, always. It was always one-upmanship. Always one brother competing against the other. That's the way we were raised."

In an emotional court appearance, Rita Musgrave testified on Tim's behalf against her fiancée Todd and described one of his rages.

"He stood up on his tiptoes," she said. "The very end of them, and his whole hands and body just became completely rigid. He couldn't coordinate. His face went into all sorts of strange looks. His eyes—his mouth was drawn down."

Three weeks into the trial, the prosecution presented a surprise witness named Arthur Santini, who stunned the courtroom with the bomb-shell that Tim had tried to hire him to murder his brother a few months earlier. The house painter claimed that Tim had offered him $5,000 to kill his twin, saying that Todd was stealing from his checking account.

Two weeks later, Tim brought up the matter again at a friend's wedding. The young millionaire, who still owed Santini money for paint, said, "I could owe you a lot more if you'd think about what I asked."

On a third occasion Tim increased his offer to $10,000, suggesting that Santini make it look like an accident. Santini testified that he had offered to murder Todd for $50,000, claiming he never actually intended to carry out the job.

Santini's stunning testimony made front-page headlines from coast to coast, even bumping the Vietnam War as that day's main television news story.

On June 7th, 1965—six months to the day after Todd's killing—Tim was found guilty of his twin brother's manslaughter. As the jury foreman read the verdict, Tim sat emotionless with his head bowed, staring into space.

"I have tried a lot of murder cases in my fourteen years on the bench," said Judge H. Burton Noble. "I think I can sum up this case by saying that it is a tragic aftermath of two emotionally disturbed youngsters receiving too much money. I think it goes without saying that we all feel sorry for this defendant. He is a victim of circumstance.''

Judge Noble sentenced Tim to serve one to ten years in jail for the manslaughter of his twin.

After serving three years at the California Institute for Men, Tim Nicholson was released on probation. Todd's fiancée Rita Musgrave visited him regularly while he was inside and they fell in love.

Five weeks after becoming a free man, Tim married Rita in the final salvo in the Nicholson twins' strange war for supremacy.

Nine

THE ROHYPNOL ROMEOS

"You spotted snakes with double tongue"
—William Shakespeare

It was a hazy, hot summer afternoon as Faith Walker stared through the coffee shop window at the boats gently bobbing at the quayside. The blonde flight attendant had a few days off between flights and had spent a leisurely afternoon shopping in Marina Del Rey, California.

As she sipped an iced cappuccino, a handsome stranger came through the front door, sat down at the next table and began smiling at her. The attractive single mother was immediately impressed by his tall, tanned, muscular body, and the coils of dark hair that fell past his broad shoulders.

She smiled back at the romantic-looking stranger, who took it as an invitation to join her.

"You've got great legs," he said in a smooth Italian accent, sitting down at her table. Thinking he was being a little too forward, even for a good-looking European, Faith said that she was late for an appointment, paid her bill and left.

But as she walked across the car lot she realized he was following close behind her.

"What's your name?" he asked with an engaging smile and a twinkle in his dark eyes. Faith hesitated by her car, won over by his sexy foreign accent and easy charm.

"Let me introduce myself," he began. "My name is Gino Sorelle and I'm an actor trying to make it in Hollywood."

He looked her straight in the eyes and she realized that she was intrigued by this persistent, handsome stranger. Just the week before she and her sister had booked an Italian vacation, and she had been reading everything about the country ever since.

"Look, this is awkward for me," he continued, "but would you like to have a real Italian dinner with a real Italian?"

Delighted by the invitation, Faith immediately accepted. Perhaps, she thought, they could share a pizza, talk about Italy and she could get some inside tips of places to go.

When he suggested meeting later that night at his apartment, she politely declined, but did agree to meet him later that week at a cozy Italian restaurant a few miles up the coast in Santa Monica.

As she drove off, she didn't notice Gino's smug smile as he congratulated himself at how well he had handled himself—and the alluring prospect of capturing another sexual victim for him and his identical twin brother.

The one word of truth he had told Faith was that he was an actor. But although he had never acted in any movie, George Spitzer was a ruthless sexual predator, who could give a near–Oscar-caliber performance when it came to chatting up women. With his brother, Stefan, who had his identical rugged good looks, George would unleash an unparalleled reign of terror on Los Angeles, leaving no young woman ever feeling safe about dating again.

Los Angeles might be the glamorous movie capital of the world, and a mecca for the beautiful people, but the Spitzer twins knew it as the perfect hunting ground for the sexual quarry they so craved. With untold thousands of lonely women desperately searching for love in the sprawling city, the Romanian-born brothers used good looks and witty charm to hook their prey, before drugging them into unconsciousness and sexually abusing them. Then they would satisfy their sexually depraved hungers together, often recording the lurid rapes on video to view triumphantly later.

Sons of two Jewish Holocaust survivors who escaped the Nazi terror by hiding out in a relative's house in Bucharest, the Spitzer twins were born in 1956 in Communist Romania. In the early seventies the government allowed their father Ladislav Spitzer to emigrate to Israel with his wife and two sons.

After failing to settle down in the Holy Land the family moved on to Greece before arriving in Canada and becoming citizens. Soon afterwards their mother died when the twins were still teenagers.

"George and Stefan were like one when they were small children," remembers Ladislav, who supported his family, working as a foreman in a textile plant in Toronto. "Nothing could ever separate them. They were happy kids. They were well brought-up, they had a good life."

After leaving school the tall, handsome brothers found jobs as salesmen for a clothing company but dreamed of going to Hollywood and becoming movie stars. They finally visited California in 1981 for a vacation and were smitten by what they viewed as a glamorous lifestyle, offering endless possibilities for success.

George and Stefan immediately returned to Toronto, quit their salesmen jobs and moved west to the Los Angeles suburb of Marina Del Rey. It wasn't long before the brothers' rugged good looks caught the attention of popular piano stylist Liberace, who immediately hired them to work for him as valets.

The brothers were delighted to be in the flamboyant superstar's entourage, believing it would lead to them meeting the right people and launch their acting careers. But their dreams were shattered when the gay pianist fired them when they spurned his lustful advances.

They then decided to concentrate on breaking into the film business and began cultivating useful contacts in Hollywood. They found jobs driving props around movie sets for a film company, attempting to talk their way into small acting roles.

Though they may have had the looks of matinee idols, the Spitzer brothers lacked any real acting talent. After a series of rejections they began to rethink their whole career strategy, deciding to concentrate on becoming movie producers, where they felt the really big money was.

Working by day as car salesmen at a Los Angeles Toyota dealership, they drove downtown at night, frequenting the nightclubs around the Sunset Strip. They shamelessly tried to cultivate anyone whom they thought could help them launch producing careers.

The big-talking twins portrayed themselves as fledgling movie moguls and always had a string of nonexistent movie projects to propose. Although they might initially impress, it wasn't long before producers realized their grandiose schemes had no substance and were just hot air.

"They were fantasists," remembers small-time movie producer Horace "Henko" Felder, whom the Spitzer brothers approached in the early 1990s to raise money for yet another film project of theirs. "It was as though they believed they should have been something huge in this town and couldn't understand why they weren't."

At first Felder believed in the brothers' proposed movie project and was interested in working with them. But he soon discovered that they didn't have a clue about the business and were totally incompetent. After a heated argument he pulled out of the project, thoroughly disillusioned.

"There was no follow-through to anything they promised," said Felder. "They were very slow to deliver and, in my experience, very quick to anger."

After almost a decade of rebuffs from the movie community, the twins became embittered with Hollywood for not recognizing their true genius. As the piles of rejection letters mounted up, their fantasies began to take a far darker path as they plotted a bizarre revenge on Hollywood.

They became obsessed with sex and the idea that they were great lovers, determining between them to bed as many beautiful Hollywood women as they could—with or without permission. Then they would film their conquests for posterity.

Ever since they were boys, George and Stefan Spitzer had had a way with women. They always seemed to have girlfriends in tow and the identical twins took a particular pride in bedding each other's lovers who often could not tell them apart.

Former girlfriends would later describe the Spitzer brothers as perfect gentlemen, with a rascally charm that could easily pull the wool over female eyes.

On a trip to Mexico they discovered a new powerful muscle relaxant called Rohypnol, which is used to calm patients before operations. The sedative—which is ten times stronger than Valium—causes temporary paralysis in patients and complete loss of memory until the effects wear off. Combined with alcohol, the effects of Rohypnol—or Roofies as the pills are popularly known—are increased dramatically. It is also extremely difficult to detect as it leaves the body so quickly.

The Spitzer brothers saw Rohypnol as their secret weapon in their quest to bed beautiful women. They brought hundreds of tablets over the border from Mexico and laid out a "swinging love nest" in their second-floor apartment in fashionable Marina Del Rey.

The failed movie actors/producers also bought video equipment to fully document their sick exploits. In their twisted minds they decided that if Hollywood wouldn't give them the opportunity to make a movie, they would produce and star in their own twisted pornographic epic, which would be called "Kisses From Romania."

During their fifteen-year career as rapists, the Spitzer brothers, together and separately, preyed on dozens of lonely women around Los Angeles. They would take them out for sumptuous meals, get them drunk and dose them with Rohypnol. Then they would drive them back to their apartment and take turns raping them while the camera rolled.

During the filming the brothers provided a full, running commentary on their perverted sex sessions. Describing themselves in their film as the "world's swingingest lovers," George and Stefan would poke fun at their hapless victims as they violated their unconscious bodies. During one scene George boasted to the camera that he had given the woman to his brother "because I couldn't be bothered to fuck her myself."

In the morning the women would wake up, heads pounding, in bed with George or Stefan and be chastised for being too drunk to remember a great night of love. They were often too embarrassed to go the police, believing that they had foolishly succumbed to the brothers' advances.

Sometimes the women willingly went to bed with the brothers, who would then pull what prosecutors later labeled the "Spitzer Switch."

One day Stefan met a beautiful brunette secretary named Brigid Rowe on the Santa Monica promenade. He asked her to join him for coffee, telling her that he was a freelance film-writer and reeling off a list of successful films he'd worked on. They exchanged telephone numbers and later went out on a date which culminated in consensual sex. Brigid fell for Stefan's looks and boyish charm and their relationship blossomed over the next few weeks.

One day she telephoned Stefan and was invited over to his apartment.

"He told me not to be alarmed when I saw him," Brigid would later testify. "[He said] he had lost weight and trimmed his body hair."

In fact George, not Stefan, had picked up the phone and, on a whim, decided to seduce his twin brother's girlfriend. When Brigid arrived at Panay Way she was amazed at how Stefan had changed in the week since she had last seen him.

Elaborating on the deception, George told her that he was in complete control of his body and had shed ten pounds by only eating fruit and vegetables.

"Every time you've seen me before I've eaten a big dinner and maybe three cheese-cakes," he claimed.

Brigid fell for his ruse and went to bed with him. It would be another two years before she realized she'd been duped.

Another young woman named Stefanie Drake also fell victim to the "Spitzer Switch" in reverse. She began a sexual relationship with

George in June 1995, after meeting him on the beach in Santa Monica. They began seeing each other regularly and then one day "George" turned up at her home, looking far heavier and hairier than when they had last been together a couple of weeks earlier. She didn't bother to ask him about it and they went to bed.

The next time she saw her Romanian lover he was back to his normal trim and hairless appearance, but on their following date he had bulked up and become hairy again.

Finally, Stefanie asked him how he managed to look so different each time. Staying cool, "George" smiled, explaining that he competed in body-building beach competitions and sometimes had to put on weight and shave his body hair.

"I'm not sure I believe you," Stefanie replied.

At this point Stefan finally admitted being George, explaining, "We are the same, we're brothers. We are the same blood."

The deviant twins had many run-ins with the police over the years, but they always managed to talk their way out of trouble. In December 1982, Stefan was charged with sodomizing twenty-nine-year-old blonde-haired Alice Henshaw, after striking up a conversation with her at the Beverly Center. They agreed to meet for drinks at the fashionable Tribeca Bar and Restaurant after which, she claimed, he raped her at his apartment.

"It was not a date-rape," claimed Stefan's lawyer Jerry Berger at his 1983 trial. "It was a one-night stand for both of them."

After a six-day trial, it took the jury just two hours to find him not guilty, and he was set free.

Both brothers were arrested in 1989 after a young woman filed a police complaint that she had been taken to George's apartment and raped. The smooth-talking twins managed to persuade detectives they didn't have a case and the district attorney's office decided not to file charges.

Two years later George was arrested in Beverly Hills after a woman claimed that he tried to forcibly undress her at his home after they met in a restaurant. She told police that George invited her out for dinner but said he had to collect his ATM card from his apartment first.

When she went upstairs to his apartment he told her to go to the closet and find a jacket to keep warm, and then suddenly grabbed her. She later testified that he lifted up her dress and proceeded to masturbate in front of her. When she began screaming he stopped, fearing neighbors would hear the commotion.

This time George was charged with battery and exposure but the trial ended in a hung jury. He eventually pleaded no contest to the battery charges in July 1995 after the other charges were dismissed. Amazingly, he was sentenced to just one day in jail and ordered to seek psychological counseling and keep away from the woman.

When Faith Walker met the man she knew as "Gino" for the date in the Italian restaurant, she immediately regretted her decision to go. George Spitzer arrived at the restaurant dressed in an open-neck, red silk shirt, with a heavy gold chain around his thick neck.

Over dinner he poured her a couple of glasses of red wine as he spun an implausible series of tall tales. As she listened in bored disbelief, he claimed that his father was the real-life model for Don Corleone, the part played by Marlon Brando in *The Godfather*; that he had once been Raquel Welch's personal trainer; and that he had a Ph.D. in psychology.

Faith didn't believe a word and resolved to make her exit at the earliest possible opportunity. At 10 p.m. she told him that she had to go home to relieve the baby-sitter who was looking after her six-year-old daughter. Then she went to the restroom and the last thing she remembered was looking at her watch and seeing that it was 10:10 p.m.

Then everything went blank and the next thing she knew she was waking up naked in his bed at 5:45 a.m. the following morning, feeling groggy and disoriented.

"Did you put something in my drink?" she

asked while George lay naked in his bed, watching her dress.

Looking genuinely shocked, he told her he would never do anything like that. He explained that they had gone back to his apartment after she developed hiccups during the meal and he had offered to give her a special remedy to cure it. Then she had passed out drunk and they had shared his bed without having sex.

"I knew something was wrong," Faith would testify later, saying that she felt sick the whole day. "I knew that I had been taken against my will."

That afternoon she went to the police and had a medical examination which showed traces of semen in her vagina, indicating that she had recently had intercourse.

A month later ten detectives from the Los Angeles Police Department raided the Spitzer brothers' Panay Way apartment after obtaining a search warrant. Inside they found an envelope containing seven boxes of Rohypnol pills and twenty-four pornographic videocassettes, some of which showed the brothers sexually assaulting their unconscious victims. They also discovered Hitachi and Panasonic video cameras and floodlights mounted on a tripod, as well as piles of photographs of naked women and two loaded revolvers.

The following day George, now forty, was arrested for investigation of drugging and kidnapping at least a dozen women and videotaping himself raping them. He was held in jail in lieu of $2 million bail and later charged with five counts of rape by use of drugs; sodomy; kidnapping for the purpose of rape; and second-degree robbery.

As detectives set up a special hot-line, appealing to other women who knew George to come forward, Stefan protested his twin brother's innocence. He claimed that Faith had consented to sex and George had only given her the Rohypnol after she asked for it to relax.

Admitting that he also appeared having sex on the seized videos, Stefan claimed that the tapes showed consensual sex recorded for "private pleasure."

By the following day the hot-line was jammed with calls from women who claimed that they were victims of the Spitzer twins.

"There is definitely more than one case building here," said LAPD Detective Carol Larcade, who lost count of the number of calls she received from angry women. "We are in the middle of a big police investigation."

In a dramatic press conference, Alice Henshaw, who had accused Stefan of raping her fourteen years earlier, tearfully appealed for other Spitzer twin victims to come forward. Eventually twenty-three women would do so.

"I'm here today because I want it to be known that I was raped by one of the Spitzer brothers," she sobbed with her back to the cameras. "I know it's hard but it'll help you, it'll help me and it'll help all the others.''

On Thursday, August 29, 1996, Stefan Spitzer was arrested and charged with one count each of rape and sodomy by drugging, attempted oral copulation while the victim was drugged, and penetration by a foreign object by drugging. His bail was set at $300,000.

''I totally deny that any of the girls in the tapes are under the influence of drugs or alcohol,'' he declared after his arrest for a 1993 rape. ''They were having a good time.''

Nine months later George and Stefan Spitzer went on trial in Los Angeles. During the three weeks of testimony the jury heard about the twins' fifteen-year reign of rape and sexual depravity.

Among the traumatized victims who testified at their trial were Faith Walker, Brigid Rowe, Stefanie Drake and Alice Henshaw. But some of the most damning testimony against the twins came from Kiki Ullman, a Swedish-born lawyer in her late twenties who had contacted detectives after the twins' arrest.

She described meeting the Spitzer brothers when they drove up to her on the street in their red convertible and asked for directions.

George explained that they had just arrived from Italy to work on a movie in Hollywood and he was lonely and homesick. As a foreigner herself, Kiki related to his plight and agreed to meet him for coffee.

Though she rejected George's attempts to

kiss her on their first date, she agreed to a second date at a chic restaurant in Brentwood. During the meal she was sipping her second glass of wine when something strange began to happen. Everything seemed to be moving in slow motion and she found herself staring at George's lips, not understanding what he was saying.

As she began to pass out she remembered him leaning forward, kissing her hard and saying, "Let's go."

The rest of the evening was like a dream. There were fuzzy images of riding in a car and George carrying her up the stairs into his bedroom and placing her on the bed. She later remembered looking down at her naked body at one point as George put on a condom and started having sex.

The following morning George was exuberant as he woke up and jumped out of bed, declaring, "This is [a] new day, life is great and I am young!"

When she asked him what had happened, George claimed they had gotten very drunk and passed out in his bed.

Kiki's story held the six-woman, six-man jury spellbound. And the twelve gasped aloud as the brothers' movie, "Kisses from Romania," was given its premiere in the courtroom. In the crudely made home movie, George Spitzer boastfully explains the "Spitzer Switch" to the camera, explaining: "Stefan's trying to dump [Debra] ... Let's see if she wants to make-up love with me instead.''

The next shot shows Debra lying naked on his bed, saying ''You look like you lost ten pounds!''

''Do you like me better now or before?'' replies a smiling George, as he moves toward the bed.

One detective who viewed all the videos said that the brothers seemed totally obsessed with having sexual power over women.

''You get the impression,'' he said, ''that when they were not filming they never stopped talking about sex.''

U.S. District Prosecutor Mary Stone said no one could ever be certain how many innocent women were sexually violated by the Spitzer brothers. She believes they carried out the drugged, rapes out of a warped sense of revenge against Hollywood, which had refused to accept them as actors and then producers.

''They picked up their victims more or less at random,'' Stone explained. ''They hung around bars, coffee shops, grocery stores, parks, subway stations—anywhere that offered the promise of an encounter.

''Some of the women they met do not know to this day whether they were raped or not. And that is a terrible mental situation for them to be in. We owe it to all their victims to put them away.''

On Wednesday, June 17, 1998, George

Spitzer was convicted of eight felonies, including kidnapping, sodomy and raping five women. He was sentenced to sixty years in prison. His brother Stefan was also found guilty of eight felony counts, including rape, sodomy, sexual battery and genital penetration by a foreign object. He received a jail term of thirty-seven years and two months.

After hearing the sentences Faith Walker said her belief in the American legal system had been restored.

"There are two more evil people off the street," she declared. "And because of us ladies, they can't hurt anyone else."

Ten

TWIN GANGSTERS

"My object all sublime, I shall achieve in time—
To make the punishment fit the crime"
—W. S. Gilbert, *The Mikado*

London in the "Swinging Sixties" will go down in history for the Beatles, the mini-skirt and the Kray twins. During their seven-year reign of terror, Ronnie and Reggie Kray introduced gangster-chic to London society, becoming the English equivalent of Chicago's infamous Al Capone in the '30s.

The identical twin murderers combined show business glamor with savage violence to etch their names in the criminal hall of infamy. As the undisputed kings of London's seamy underworld, their lucrative criminal empire included gambling, protection rackets and drugs. While mixing socially with the Beatles, Judy Garland and movie star George Raft, the ruthlessly ambitious Krays forged links with the American Mafia, hell-bent on criminal world domination.

They placed themselves above the law and would ultimately pay a terrible price for their despicable crimes.

*   *   *

The Kray twins were born into poverty in the tough working-class district of Hoxton in London on October 24, 1933. Reggie was just ten minutes older than Ronnie. Even as babies there was an uncanny telepathic link between the twins. One always knew what the other was thinking and from the very beginning they shared a love of violence.

"I was born to be violent," Reggie Kray would boast many years later.

At the age of eleven the twins, who were physically impossible to tell apart, were taught to box by their elder brother, Charlie, who was already a Navy champion. Life on the mean streets of London's East End was tough and the twins' mother, Violet, often had to pawn jewelry in order to put food on the table. It was left to Violet to bring up the twins, as their father, Charles, refused to serve his country at the outbreak of World War II and went into hiding for twelve years.

From childhood the Kray twins learned to hate the police from the constant raids on their house, searching for their deserter father. They saw the law as *the* enemy and it wasn't long before they got into trouble when they started a street gang. Reggie was the first to be arrested when he was caught firing his new air pistol out of a train window.

As teenagers they entered boxing competitions, once even fighting each other in a memorable bout, with Reggie winning on points. They also made extra pocket money by fighting in illegal street prize fights.

The twins delighted in fooling their teachers at Daniel Street School, impersonating each other whenever one got into trouble. It was a game that they would use to their advantage with police and prison wardens throughout their criminal career.

When they were sixteen the Kray twins fought a savage gang war, arming themselves with bike chains and other weapons. After beating up three other teenagers they were both arrested for grievous bodily harm and were tried at the Old Bailey, where they were acquitted after a friendly priest spoke out on their behalf.

A year later they weren't so lucky when the twins beat up a policeman. They found themselves back in court and were jailed for a month. Their reputation as the "fastest guns in the East End" was now firmly secured.

In 1954 the twins turned twenty-one and formed the Kray Gang, composed of local hoodlums. They bought a run-down billiard hall in Mile End, London, and made it their headquarters. They organized a lucrative protection racket, charging owners of local pubs, shops and businesses hard cash in exchange for a peaceful existence.

The twins also bought an arsenal of firearms which they didn't hesitate to use against enemies.

"We were fearless in those days," Reggie Kray would later recall. "Fighting was our game."

Every night the Kray Gang went out drinking and looking for trouble. When a rival gang called the Maltese Boys tried to muscle into their territory the Krays soundly ran them out of town at gunpoint.

Almost overnight the Krays' illegal enterprises started paying off, and, fired with an ambition to become the kings of London's underworld, they began their move into the big time.

In the mid-1950s, London was one big party as the country recovered from the effects of World War II, enjoying a new economic lease on life. With war rationing finally over there was money to spend and people flocked into the West End drinking clubs every night to enjoy themselves.

The twins gained their first foothold in the West End when they made a deal with the owner of a drinking club called Stragglers. In return for clearing out troublemakers who were terrorizing the club, Ronnie and Reggie were given a partnership and a piece of the action.

But when a rival gang beat up the club owner, Ronnie Kray and two of his gang members retaliated in a bloody battle, leaving one man seriously hurt. Ronnie was jailed for two years for his part in the attack but soon turned it to his advantage by setting himself up as Wandsworth Prison's biggest tobacco baron and reaping big profits.

A proud, self-confessed homosexual, Ronnie Kray began to believe that other inmates were plotting to murder him and began getting an uncontrollable urge to kill. He was declared insane by the prison's psychiatrist and was institutionalized in a mental hospital outside London.

His twin brother Reggie, worried that Ronnie might be locked up for the rest of his life as mentally ill, planned his escape. During a hospital visit the identical twins swapped clothes in a toilet and Ronnie calmly walked out to freedom. Thirty minutes later Reggie told the duty officer that he was leaving, and produced his driving license to prove his identity. After an hour of questioning he was allowed to leave and the Kray twins were back in business.

"It's amazing how easy it is to deceive the authorities," said Ronnie. "Particularly if you've got the nerve—and a twin brother,"

A few weeks later Ronnie returned to the hospital and, after being declared sane, returned to prison to serve out his sentence.

While his brother was behind bars Reggie bought an empty, run-down shop near Bow police station and transformed it into a high-class drinking and illegal gambling establishment. Naming it "The Double R," after the twins, he built a stage and dance area and attempted to create a family atmosphere.

At The Double R, the Kray twins found themselves mixing with London's rich and famous. They befriended the top celebrities of the day, including movie stars Barbara Windsor and Diana Dors and veteran Hollywood tough guy George Raft.

When Ronnie was released from prison he immediately joined Reggie as co-host at their new club. The Krays were on hand every night, welcoming guests, dressed in their handmade matching midnight-blue suits and colorful bow ties. The genial gangster twins were naturals for the thriving West End club circuit, charming their way into the rich society crowd who frequented it.

"They were very courtly to meet," said the English writer and social historian Anthony Hayden-Guest, who became friends with Ronnie Kray during this period. "Although they didn't come over as crazy people, you wouldn't want to hang around with these guys outside."

The Kray twins loved rubbing shoulders with millionaires, movie stars and aristocrats and delighted in having their pictures with celebrities appear in newspaper society columns. And they were fast becoming famous in their own right.

But lying beneath their new-found respectability, the twins didn't neglect their thriving underworld enterprises, which included fencing stolen property, drugs and loan-sharking.

After the police closed down The Double R for not having a proper license, the Krays decided to go even more up-market with a new club called "The Kentucky" on Mile End Road, Stepney. Spending thousands of dollars on red plush carpets, expensive furniture and mirrored walls, it soon became *the* club to go to in London.

The rich and famous were fascinated with the Krays and their tough gangster friends. The Kentucky was like an underworld-themed club, and they could visit the wild side without ever putting themselves at risk.

Willingly paying outrageous prices for food and drink, and then losing their money gambling, London's high society flocked to the club for an exhilarating night out, lining the Krays' pockets at the same time.

"This was a period in London when gangster-chic became very fashionable," said Hayden-Guest. "The upper-classes were so impregnated with snobbery that they got a sinister thrill from mixing with dangerous people who they felt did not endanger them."

The twins were delighted when director Joan Littlewood chose the Kentucky to shoot key scenes for the movie. *Sparrows Can't Sing*, starring their friend Barbara Windsor. After attending the film premiere with their parents, the Kray twins hosted a party to celebrate. Their guests included Princess Margaret's husband Lord Snowdon, film star Roger Moore and photographer David Bailey. "I felt so powerful that night," remembered Reggie fondly.

For a brief moment in so-called Swinging Sixties London, the high-life and low-life came together as the Kray twins stamped their unique mark on the city's nightlife. But the police were not amused and in 1964 they closed down the club for illegal drinking and gambling.

But a year later the Krays were back with a new club called Esmerelda's Barn in fashionable Knightsbridge. This time they craftily involved the establishment by recruiting a real-life aristocrat, Lord Effingham, onto their board of directors.

The hot new club took the Krays into a new league. It made them millionaires in their own right, as fortunes were won and lost on their gaming tables every night. To capitalize on their success the twins fanned out over England, buying clubs in Birmingham and Leicester. They brought over top American entertainers and sportsmen like the World Heavyweight Boxing champion Sonny Liston and the legendary Joe Louis to make guest appearances at their clubs.

They also forged lasting friendships with superstars like Judy Garland and George Raft, who happily provided free public relations by being photographed with the Krays.

On one memorable occasion Judy Garland took the twins to a West End club and introduced them to the Beatles, who happened to be there that night. They shared a table and Ronnie Kray and John Lennon got on excellently, discovering they were kindred spirits.

In 1966 Ronnie decided to take the Kray Gang international by courting the American Mafia with the idea of launching a trans-Atlantic crime syndicate. Using their underworld connections, the Krays set up a top-level crime summit meeting in Brooklyn and Ronnie flew over to meet a top New York Mafioso.

"The atmosphere was electric," Ronnie Kray would later recall. "I knew I was in the big leagues and I'd better make out a good case for being here, otherwise these bastards were liable to chop my balls off."

After the initial tension the New York mobster warmed to the London crime boss, warning him that Scotland Yard had tipped off the FBI and he was being watched. Over the next few days they discussed many joint enterprises like flying rich gamblers from Las Vegas to London for week-long gambling orgies at the Krays' clubs.

"It was a whole exciting new world for Ron and me," said Reggie Kray. "Suddenly we could see a different direction to go in."

When Ronnie returned to London at the end of the week he was convinced he would make criminal history by forging an historic link between the Kray Gang and the American Mafia. But after months of negotiations, the Mafia finally pulled out as they realized the instability of the Kray twins. The Mafia saw their criminal empire as a mere castle in the sand that could be washed away at any moment. And they didn't want any involvement.

"The American Dream never quite came off for Reggie and me," Ronnie would remember philosophically. "Although we did do some business with the Mafia."

The Kray twins' love of publicity would ultimately lead to their spending the rest of their lives behind bars. When Ronnie Kray was innocently photographed in deep conversation with Lord Boothby, a top Conservative peer at the time, the Fleet Street tabloids erroneously claimed the two were having a homosexual affair.

The *Sunday Mirror* printed a story claiming that Scotland Yard was investigating the relationship between "a prominent peer" and a "leading thug in the London underworld." The article also mentioned them both attending wild Mayfair parties and making illicit trips to Brighton.

Although Lord Boothby successfully sued the newspaper for libel and won £40,000 in damages, the seeds of the Krays' downfall were sown. Scotland Yard now viewed the famous gangster twins as a direct threat to the English establishment, and began an investigation into their activities. Two top police detectives were assigned full-time to probe the Kray twins and find the evidence to send them to jail.

But as Ronnie and Reggie Kray became richer and more powerful they believed they were invincible and began making serious mistakes as they veered out of control.

Ronnie Kray's uncontrollable depressions and rages, which had once led to him being certified as insane, could turn violent at the slightest provocation. He often believed that friends and family alike were plotting against him, and his paranoia knew no bounds.

On one occasion he found out that his male croupier boyfriend was having an affair with a friend of his. Ronnie Kray went berserk, cutting the unfortunate man from ear to ear as he was hung upside down outside his bedroom window. Although he survived, others were less fortunate when they crossed Ronnie.

George Cornell was the leading hit man for the Krays' main rivals, the Richardson Gang, who operated a criminal fiefdom across the River Thames in south London. During the Krays' negotiations with the Mafia, the two London gangs had met in secret at the Astor Club to discuss an alliance to avoid any potential London gang war that would put off the Americans.

During the meeting Cornell sealed his death warrant when he launched a personal attack on Ronnie Kray, calling him "a big, fat poof." Ronnie was furious, vowing to kill Cornell with his own hands at the earliest opportunity.

Four months later he had his chance when Cornell led the Richardson Gang in an armed attack on a club where they thought the Krays would be drinking. Although the twins were not there at the time, a close friend and fellow Kray gang member was shot to death during the fracas.

The following night, March 9, 1966, Ronnie Kray heard that Cornell was drinking in the Blind Beggar public house on Whitechapel Road, right in the middle of the Kray Gang territory. This was the final insult for Ronnie, who loaded his favorite 9-mm Mauser automatic and drove straight to the Blind Beggar, picking up one of his henchmen on the way.

When they arrived at the gloomy old pub it was almost deserted. There were three customers drinking by the bar and a barmaid and an old man at a nearby table. Sitting at the far end of the bar was George Cornell, who was tapping his foot to the jukebox as it played the popular Walker Brothers' hit of the day, "The Sun Ain't Gonna Shine Any More."

Ronnie calmly walked over, took out his gun and aimed it straight at Cornell's face. Then without saying a word he pulled the trigger at point-blank range, sending the gangster falling to the bar with blood pouring from his head. Cornell was dead by the time he hit the floor.

Witnessing the killing, the horrified customers and barmaid ran for their lives out of the pub, as Ronnie Kray calmly returned the gun to his shoulder holster and walked out nonchalantly, as if nothing had happened.

"I felt fucking marvelous," Ronnie would later recall. "I have never felt so good, so bloody alive, before or since."

As he got into his car and drove off, Ronnie knew that none of the witnesses would dare talk to police for fear of the Krays. He believed he was so powerful that he could get away with murder at will. He felt unstoppable. Again and again in later years he would relive the Cornell killing, getting an almost orgasmic thrill from the memory.

For the next couple of years it seemed that Ronnie Kray's boast about being able to get away with murder had been correct. Although Scotland Yard knew he had shot down George Cornell in cold blood in public, no one was brave enough to come forward and squeal on the Krays.

But eighteen months later his twin brother Reggie committed his own murder to put himself on an equal footing with his brother, and sealed the Krays' fate forever.

Jack "The Hat" McVitie was a small-time gangster with a big mouth who worked part-time as an enforcer for the Kray Gang. The self-conscious gangster, who always wore a hat to hide his baldness, fell afoul of Reggie Kray after messing up several jobs through drink and drugs, endangering the twins' criminal empire.

On one occasion Reggie took McVitie with him to a club owner to collect $1,500 protection money that the Krays were owed. The owner asked for more time to pay, saying he could only manage $300 as he was broke. Although Reggie agreed to give him more time, McVitie suddenly pulled out his gun and shot the owner in the foot. It was left to Reggie to clear up the mess by arranging for an underworld doctor to treat his wounds.

A few weeks later McVitie upset Reggie even more when he was caught red-handed stealing Kray drug profits and later boasting about it.

But the final straw came when McVitie staggered drunkenly into a club, brandishing a sawed-off shotgun and screaming that he was going to kill the twins. When Reggie heard about the incident he was furious, deciding to make an example of McVitie and send a clear message to the underworld that the Kray twins still ruled London.

Arming himself with a .32 automatic, Reggie rounded up his brother and some trusted gang members and went in search of McVitie. When they arrived at the club he was supposed to be in, McVitie had already left. Then, by accident, they ran into him in a nearby Chinese restaurant.

When he saw the Krays walk in, McVitie, who was drunk, began threatening to kill them again. Then he staggered out without paying the bill.

Later that night the Krays tricked McVitie into attending a party they were going to. As he walked through the door, Reggie calmly came over, took out his gun and aimed it straight at McVitie's head. When the gun jammed, McVitie started pleading for his life before suddenly running across the room and trying to dive through the window.

Ronnie soon caught up with McVitie and brought him back, holding his arms securely behind his back. The terrified villain was shaking with fear as Ronnie Kray told him to be a man and take his punishment.

Then somebody handed Reggie a long carving knife from the kitchen. Holding a drink in one hand and the knife in the other, Reggie gave McVitie a long icy stare. Without saying a word, he pushed the knife slowly into McVitie's eye before repeatedly stabbing him in the face and throat until he stopped screaming.

Finally satisfied that McVitie was dead, Reggie left the party, ordering his henchmen to clear up the bloody mess and dispose of McVitie's body, which hasn't been found to this day.

"I felt relieved and a bit sick," Reggie would later remember in his memoirs. "I felt bad afterwards, though. I had a lot of nightmares."

*   *   *

On May 9, 1968, Scotland Yard finally caught up with the thirty-four-year-old Kray twins and arrested them for murder. Several members of their gang, who faced long prison sentences for other crimes, decided to testify against the twins in return for immunity.

As the Kray twins and their brother Charlie, who was arrested as an accomplice in the murder of Jack McVitie, awaited trial in Brixton Prison, their empire fell to pieces. Friend after friend turned against them.

At first the twins were convinced they would soon be free and hired the most expensive lawyers to fight their case. Every day their devoted mother Violet brought them a home-made lunch and a bottle of wine to wash it down with. But as their Old Bailey trial neared and the evidence against them mounted, they realized their chances were slim.

"We decided we would go down with dignity and style," explained Ronnie.

The Kray twins entered the dock at the Old Bailey in January 1969 in what Fleet Street billed as "The Trial of the Century." Their thirty-nine-day murder trial turned into a huge public spectacle with black-market tickets to the public gallery being sold outside for excessive prices.

The Krays' old friend Judy Garland sent a good luck telegram and Hollywood movie star Charlton Heston, who was fascinated by the case, attended much of the trial.

In the end just three lieutenants in the Kray Gang stayed loyal to their leaders, the rest turning Queen's evidence against them. The full weight of the English establishment came down on the twins and after the jury pronounced them guilty on March 8, the judge did not hesitate to voice his contempt.

"I am not going to waste words on you," declared Mr. Justice Melford-Stevenson. "I sentence you to life imprisonment, which I recommend should not be less than thirty years." Their elder brother Charles was sentenced to ten years.

On March 17, 1995, after serving exactly twenty-six years of his sentence, Ronnie Kray collapsed and died of a heart attack at Broadmoor Mental Hospital, where he had been transferred from jail after being declared insane. At his funeral, which brought traffic to a halt in the East End, his distraught twin brother Reggie broke down in tears as his final message to Ronnie was read out.

It said: "My brother, Ron, is now free and at peace. Ron had great humor, a vicious temper, was kind and generous. He did it all his way, but above all he was a man. That's how I will always remember my twin brother, Ron. God bless. Affection, Reg."

Reggie Kray, now sixty-five years old, is still serving his sentence at Maidstone Prison. He was denied parole in 1998 and looks set to die behind bars.

Eleven

THE COOKIE LADIES

"Sisterhood is powerful"
—Robin Morgan, 1970

Twin sisters Dorthea and Mary Margaret Beck shared their lives for sixty-eight years and were inseparable. Born in the same single-story white-picket-fenced house bought by their grandparents at the turn of the century, they attended school together before getting identical jobs in the same hospital, where they worked until they retired.

The four-foot eleven-inch, never-married twins brought a ray of sunshine into their small town with their kindness and generosity. Known as "the Cookie Ladies" for the chocolate chip treats they baked to give to local children, the Beck twins had been cherished pillars of their Alton, Illinois, community for several generations.

As they drove their battered old car to the local supermarket with their pet poodle, Pepper, the diminutive sisters cut striking figures. Every day like clockwork, Dorthea and Mary would hand out bags of freshly baked cookies to the children in the street and chat to anyone who passed by. They seemed a unique slice of Americana come to life, dispatching kind words of advice and homespun wisdom.

Every Sunday the elderly twins, who resembled an identical pair of Grandma Moseses with their large, black framed spectacles and matching smiles, would don their best clothes and walk through Alton to attend the Evangelical United Church. Sitting in the front pew together, they enthusiastically led the congregation in singing their favorite hymns.

After service they would discuss the sermon on the church steps, trading local gossip with their neighbors and waxing lyrically about the good old days before the neighborhood became run-down and riddled with crime.

But behind ''the Cookie Ladies' '' genial smiles and mumsiness lay a dreadful secret which would finally explode in gruesome murder, shocking the entire town of Alton to its very foundations.

The Beck twins were the third generation of their family to live in the white wooden house at 1420 Highland Avenue, Alton. Born on January 28, 1927, to a meatpacker, the chubby-faced twin sisters always dressed identically and were impossible to tell apart.

Growing up, they lived in their own world, attending Alton High School where they were both near the top of their class. And even as young girls their easygoing charm and friendliness ensured their popularity with their classmates.

In the 1930s and 1940s Alton was a prosperous old Mississippi River town, attracting middle-class Chicago business people wanting to escape the hustle and bustle of the big city. With its picturesque views of the winding Mississippi River and its fresh country air, Alton provided the perfect antidote to the stress of city life.

Like many other Irish immigrants, the twins' grandfather moved to Alton at the beginning of the century, settling into the modest house in one of the many bluff-top neighborhoods that dotted the town.

Dorthea and Mary grew up working-class with strict religious values instilled in them. It was a noisy house and their parents were loud and ebullient often arguing passionately late into the night. The boisterous atmosphere in which they were raised would rub off on the twins, who always enjoyed a good argument.

''They just talked loud,'' said an old friend of the twins. ''Their mother did too. They were raised that way.''

Both sisters loved the simple down-to-earth life in Alton, and it never entered their heads to leave the town like their younger sister, who moved to St. Louis after marriage.

When their parents died and left them the house, Dorthea and Mary both found jobs at

Alton Memorial Hospital to support themselves as X-ray assistants, never considering leaving the house they had been born in. While their friends married and raised families, the Beck twins showed no interest in dating and seemed inseparable, enjoying one another's company and relying on each other for everything.

While many of their neighbors considered them odd and eccentric, they adored them and over the years the sisters became a much-loved institution in Alton.

Even as young women they seemed frumpy and middle-aged, forsaking fashionable clothes for plainer, more sensible garments to see them through the cold, hard Illinois winters. And the years did little to change the twins. While Dorthea gained a lot of weight and began dyeing her hair black, Mary stayed thin and let her hair gray naturally, wearing it in a simple bob.

Although Alton changed beyond recognition in the 1950s and 1960s, as local industry moved out and plunged the town into bankruptcy, the Beck twins seemed to be the one constant factor that everyone could rely on.

Their seventy-four-year-old best friend and neighbor, Alma Jarrett, who knew the twins for more than half a century, said they were a rock.

''They were perfect neighbors,'' said Alma. ''They were somebody I could call and knew they would be there all the time.''

Every day the twins would stop by at Alma's house to chat and discuss their favorite television programs. Dorthea would always volunteer to fetch her supplies from the store, refusing to take any money although they always struggled to make ends meet.

Bill Haine—later to become Madison County State Attorney—grew up three blocks away from the Becks and knew them well as a child. "Everybody liked them and they were always giving us kids cookies they'd baked," he remembered. "They loved children and I'd always see them in the market. They were just two kind elderly ladies."

But after they retired from the hospital when they reached sixty-five, a sinister new dynamic entered the twins' relationship. Dorthea had always been more dominant than the easy-going Mary, but suddenly their relationship turned abusive.

The tiny sisters had always bickered and argued in private, but after retirement the rows became far more heated and often public. Without having jobs and a purpose in life, the Beck sisters started becoming secretive and reclusive, spending most of their time at home arguing.

Suddenly they stopped baking their cookies, to the great disappointment of the children, and withdrew into themselves, only venturing out for groceries.

Although they attended church every Sunday, still taking an active part in religious activities, they hardly ever spoke to anyone. Their kind smiles were replaced by constant scowls as they looked disapprovingly at each other, Dorthea finding fault with everything her twin sister did.

When Eddie and Jacquette Anderson bought a two-story brick house next door to the Becks in 1991, they were warned beforehand that their new neighbors liked to argue. As both sisters became increasingly hard of hearing they began shouting louder and louder at each other.

"They kept to themselves," said Eddie Anderson. "They liked watching my daughter play on the swing between our houses and they always had a kind word for her. They were nice old ladies and decent neighbors. But there were growing problems which unfortunately no one recognized until it was too late."

Over the next two years the twins' constant screaming and shouting got worse, leading some to fear that their arguments had turned violent. Their daily bickering grew so heated that neighbors began to question whether they should call the police or social services to investigate.

For some years Mary had had high blood pressure and was on medication prescribed by her doctor. But in June 1995, she suddenly seemed to lose the will to live, announcing that she no longer wanted to take her pills. Dorthea was terrified of losing her twin, not being able to face the prospect of being alone for the first time in her life. So she began a bizarre campaign to cruelly punish Mary for daring to leave her.

During the summer of 1995 Dorthea vented her frustration at her ailing twin sister's refusal to go to the doctor by battering her. She beat her black-and-blue from head to toe with her hands and her walking cane, as she screamed at her to see the doctor for her bad heart.

Every night neighbors would hear shouting and screaming as Dorthea launched a tirade of abuse. And as Mary's health declined to the point where she was too sick to leave the house, Dorthea's beatings became even worse.

Without Mary at her side Dorthea stopped going out of the house, refusing to be seen alone without her twin sister. For the first time in living memory the Beck twins' favorite church pew lay empty at Sunday services and Dorthea now had their food delivered from their favorite supermarket. She would appear at the front door alone to sign for it always refusing to allow anyone into the house.

When concerned friends and neighbors telephoned to offer help, Dorthea always answered the phone. She would thank them for their kindness, saying that Mary was feeling a little under the weather and she was nursing her.

By November Mary had stopped eating altogether and Dorthea tried everything to make her sister take nourishment as she lost weight. She begged and cajoled Mary to eat her freshly cooked meals, and when she refused, Dorthea beat her sister even harder.

Dorthea, who was becoming senile, was now at the end of her tether. Having abandoned all hopes of making Mary eat, she began to consider murder to punish her twin sister for being so difficult and disruptive.

On Monday, November 20, 1995, Dorthea Beck had reached the breaking point. It had been a long, torturous weekend for Dorthea, who at one point had gotten so frustrated by her ailing sister taking so long to walk across the room, that she'd thrown Mary's walker at the front door and broken the glass.

Mary had given up trying to resist her sister's bullying and had lost the will to fight back and defend herself. She weighed just 98 pounds and was wasting away from chronic malnutrition.

After watching the 7 o'clock evening news on television, Dorthea went into the kitchen to fetch the evening meal she had prepared. As usual she set out a portion for Mary, who hobbled into the kitchen with her cane to sit down at the table for another meal she wouldn't eat.

As Dorthea tried to force a spoonful of food down her mouth, Mary defiantly spat the food straight in her sister's face. Suddenly all the years of rage and frustration with her twin came to a furious boil as Dorthea snapped. The bigger, more powerful twin picked up Mary's walking stick and hit her squarely across the forehead, breaking her glasses and sending her false teeth rattling across the floor.

As Mary fell to the ground screaming in agony, Dorthea flew into a frenzy, raining heavy blows down on her sister's head and body with the cane. Then she started kicking Mary repeatedly in the face and chest, breaking several ribs, not stopping until her sister lay dead in a pool of blood.

Pausing to catch her breath, Dorthea looked down on her dead twin and breathed a sigh of relief. Then she calmly sat down near her body and began plotting an alibi to get away with murder.

Nearly two hours later, at 10 p.m., Dorthea got up from her chair and walked over to the cupboard to clean up the blood-soaked kitchen. The heavyset old lady carefully picked up her sister's broken glasses and false teeth, placing them in the sink to wash. She then undressed Mary, taking off her blood-soaked clothes, and began to bathe the numerous cuts and bruises covering her sister's entire body. Carefully wiping the blood off Mary's false teeth, she forced open her sister's jaw to fit them back in place.

After dragging Mary's body to the corner of the kitchen, Dorthea began washing down the floor to get rid of the evidence. Over the next few hours she methodically cleaned the entire kitchen, putting everything back in its proper place, so there would be no signs of the murderous struggle. Finally she hid Mary's blood-stained nightgown and the cleaning towel in a box on the back porch.

It was almost dawn when she dressed Mary in her pale blue nightgown and dragged her back to the center of the kitchen, placing her head on a pillow as if she were asleep.

Then Dorthea calmly walked into the bedroom she shared with Mary. Sinking down on her bed, exhausted, she had a few hours' sleep to prepare herself for the ordeal ahead.

At 7.30 a.m. Dorthea rubbed the sleep from her eyes as she slowly got out of bed. Looking across at her sister's empty bed, she mulled over the events of the previous night and felt no remorse. It was the start of a new life alone without Mary, who was always spoiling things and upsetting her.

For the first time in her sixty-eight years, Dorthea felt like herself; she had finally cut herself adrift from her anchor of a twin sister. Now there would be no one to hold her back.

As she walked past the kitchen into the parlor, she saw her sister's body lying on the floor with the pillow under her battered head. Mary looked strangely peaceful, as if she were asleep and having wonderful dreams, thought Dorthea. It was all for the best.

Reaching for the phone, Dorthea dialed 911, calmly telling the operator that her sister had passed on in her sleep and to send an ambulance. Then she telephoned her old friend Alma Jarrett, saying she'd found Mary on the floor dead but everything was all right as she had already called police and paramedics.

When Alton homicide detectives Chris Sullivan and Michael Gordon arrived at the twins' Highland Avenue house a few minutes later, they were met by the Becks' neighbor, Tracy Henderson, who led them into the kitchen. There they found Dorthea leaning over her sister's dead body, as if in deep contemplation.

"Mary's died," she announced calmly, not seeming the slightest bit distressed.

As the detectives recoiled in horror, Dorthea pointed a stubby finger at Mary Beck's bruised and battered body, which lay covered in a white sheet.

"Mary was so tired last night that she wanted to sleep on the floor, so I let her," she explained matter-of-factly.

Detective Gordon was stunned as he lifted the sheet and noticed that Mary's frail, emaciated body was covered in cuts and heavy bruising. Although it immediately appeared obvious that the old lady had died from a savage beating, it seemed strange that the wounds had been recently cleaned and there were no signs of bleeding.

As he checked for vital signs, Dorthea explained how she had awakened and discovered Mary lying unconscious. After unsuccessfully trying to wake her up, she realized that her sister was dead and summoned help.

Dorthea told Sullivan and Gordon how her sister had been neglecting food and medication over the last few weeks. Suddenly she was overtaken by anger, astonishing the detectives by accusing Mary of killing herself by refusing to eat and take her medicines.

It seemed an unlikely scenario and police immediately suspected murder. But the idea that one elderly twin sister would cold-bloodedly murder the other was almost beyond the realm of human comprehension.

"Dorthea did not appear distraught or sad about her sister's passing in the least," said the chief investigator for Madison County Coroner's Office, Ralph Baahlmann, Jr., who arrived at the house soon afterward. "It just didn't fit and her explanation seemed rather odd. We were just not accepting her argument."

Later that morning at Alton police headquarters, Dorthea Beck seemed visibly nervous as she stuck to her story. Appearing evasive and uncomfortable, the elderly spinster answered the investigator's questions succinctly, appearing oddly cold and indifferent to her twin sister's death.

Eventually, under Baahlmann's tough questioning, Dorthea broke down, confessing the terrible truth. Under oath she admitted beating Mary and striking her numerous times until she'd fallen to the floor. Then she'd kicked her to death.

But amazingly, even now Dorthea showed no signs of remorse for murdering her twin.

"She did not cry or weep," said Baahlmann. "These were twin sisters who had lived together for sixty-eight years and one would have thought that perhaps she would have been somewhat more emotional. At no point did she express any sorrow or emotion that she was saddened by her sister's death."

That night Dorthea Beck was formally arraigned and charged with the first-degree murder of her twin sister, and locked up in Madison County Jail without bail.

When local newspapers broke the news that one of "the Cookie Ladies" had murdered the other, the entire town of Alton was horrified. It seemed inconceivable that the nice little old lady whom the town had loved for years could torture and murder her twin sister so barbarically.

"I was totally shocked," said Madison County State's Attorney Bill Haine, who had grown up with the Beck twins and would lead the prosecution team. "It's a special tragedy and this extraordinary homicide shocked the whole community. They were both well-liked and everyone here felt a personal loss."

Two days after the murder, dressed in a prison regulation orange jumpsuit, Dorthea appeared before a judge at the Madison County Courthouse. Calm and even talkative, the senior-citizen killer told Judge Charles Romani, Jr., that she couldn't afford an attorney and requested a public defender.

Not a flicker of emotion crossed the old lady's jowly face as the judge told her that she faced up to sixty years in jail, if found guilty.

"If convicted," said Judge Romani, "the minimum time you will do is twenty years. The new statute in this state no longer allows [time off for good behavior]. That means if you are sentenced to twenty years, you will serve twenty years."

In November 1996, Dorthea Beck was found unfit to stand trial and was placed in the custody of the Illinois Department of Mental Health and Development Disabilities for an indefinite period.

Public defender Neil Hawkins said that Dorthea would probably spend the rest of her life in the state mental hospital.

"Senile dementia had set in," he explained. "I think she just went off the deep end and she has no memory of her sister's death. She was just in her own little world."

Twelve

THE GIFT OF DEATH

"When all the world dissolves, And every creature shall be purified, All places shall be hell that is not heaven"

—Christopher Marlowe
— *The Tragical History of Doctor Faustus*
[1604]

Janie Deitriech picked up the almost-empty whiskey bottle and poured the last drop. She felt numb from the muscle relaxants she had been taking and wanted nothing more than to sink into oblivion. It would make everything so much easier.

She looked over at her twin sister, Genie, who lay unconscious on the couch. There had been a time, growing up, that everybody had said they looked alike. But as Janie tried to focus on the bloated, middle-aged woman in front of her, she wondered if she really looked as bad.

Janie had always loved Genie more than anything in the world. Their childhood had been a nightmare; an ordeal they had survived together to give them a special, enduring bond beyond even twinship. She could still remember those long, dark nights when their stepfather had beaten them and then satisfied his perverse cravings.

Janie had always known exactly what her twin was thinking without having to ask. They didn't need words to communicate and even when they were thousands of miles apart she always knew when Genie was sick or unhappy. Later she would always be proved right.

Staggering over to the record player, Janie put on another blues album and gazed lovingly at her sister. Genie looked so peaceful lying there—so helpless. Why couldn't things have been different?

Realizing it was the end of their long, dark road together, Janie brushed a tear away with a handkerchief as she tried to clear her cloudy head from the effects of the whiskey and pills.

The twins had certainly not had an easy life. Janie had always envied their smiling friends, who seemed to sail effortlessly through happy marriages and kids without a care in the world. The forty-six-year-old sisters had certainly picked short straws and it had only gotten worse as they grew older, their lives paralleling each other in misery and heartbreak.

They'd both gotten pregnant at fifteen and found themselves on their own. After brief, unhappy marriages to other men, who had come to their rescue, they'd stumbled through a string of broken romances, having babies who were always put up for adoption as the twins were unable to care for them. Their only real escape had been drugs and drink; a brief vacation away from the horrors of their lives. But they'd always had to come down to earth the next morning.

Suicide had been an option but, though they'd tried to resist as good Catholics, they'd each made several attempts. They might be damned in this life but they were scared of going to purgatory.

Genie had really died five years earlier, when her beloved son, Sam, had been murdered and she'd watched in court as his killers got away with it almost scot-free. Since then she'd lost the will to live and sunk ever further into the abyss. Now all Genie wanted to do was take her pills and sleep.

Three months earlier, when Genie's husband walked out, Janie had gotten so worried about her twin that she'd insisted Genie move into her apartment so as not to be alone.

"We really know the blues," sighed Janie to herself as she listened to the mournful Delta blues record which seemed to be playing the soundtrack to their lives.

She reached over to the bottle to pour another drink but suddenly remembered it was empty. Then, knocking her glass to the floor, she lit a cigarette, trying to focus on the flickering match flame dancing in front of her. It reminded her of being a little girl and lighting cigarettes for her stepfather. Sadly that had been the only real bond between them. Maybe that's why fire had always fascinated her so much. She loved to see a match gaily spark into a flame, enthralled by all that power and possibility.

That Sunday, Genie had reached an all-time low. A week earlier she had taken an overdose of pills but had been revived in time, and then threatened to kill herself at the earliest opportunity. Janie knew it was only a matter of time before she succeeded, but had thought of another way for her sister to find eternal peace without damning her soul.

Picking up the Bible they had both been reading earlier, before the drink and pills had taken their toll, she felt instantly comforted. As little girls they had both loved to read the Bible, finding a calm reassurance in the beautiful stories inside.

''The Lord is my strength and song, and is become my salvation,'' she read aloud from the book of Genesis.

Placing the book by her sister's head, Janie prepared herself. She had never let Genie down so far and never would. Killing her out of love would be the true test of their twinship—the ultimate gift.

''I must be strong,'' she said out loud, finding a curious strength and resolve in the words.

Walking across the room she felt weightless, like an astronaut in space, as she picked up a stack of newspapers and magazines, carefully placing them next to Genie's unconscious body. Then, taking one final look at the twin she loved so deeply, she knelt down and tenderly kissed her on the forehead.

"Please, God, give me strength," Janie murmured as she lit a match, touched it to a newspaper and dropped it on the magazines, watching them catch fire. Muttering long-forgotten prayers under her breath she moved effortlessly over to the window and watched in a strangely detached mixture of fascination and horror as the fire took hold.

Within seconds the flames were licking at Genie's nightdress but her twin never cried out as they began to consume her.

"She won't feel a thing," thought Janie. "And she'll go straight to heaven."

Janie and Genie Cerullo were born in 1950 in the untamed backwoods of Cranberry, West Virginia. Their father was a coal miner but lack of work forced him to move the family north to the more prosperous city of Hamilton, Ohio, while they were still infants.

Soon after they arrived their parents had another daughter, Susie, but the marriage collapsed in divorce when their father walked out. The twins and their baby sister stayed with their mother, Thelma, who soon remarried.

Janie and Genie were inseparable from the beginning with an almost mystical bond between them that seemed to defy explanation.

"It was amazing," remembers their younger sister, Susie Cerullo. "They could feel each other's pain. One of them always knew when there was something wrong with the other.''

Money was tight and it was a very difficult childhood for the three girls, who were living with four half-brothers from their mother's new marriage.

Their stepfather was a tyrant who beat and sexually abused the girls, leaving a legacy of pain that would scar their lives forever. Thelma, who was dependent on the amphetamines she was prescribed for a serious thyroid condition which caused drastic weight fluctuations, was seriously depressed and unable to protect her children.

''Our childhoods were not good,'' said Susie. ''We were all emotionally and physically abused.''

At school the painfully shy twins were cruelly mocked and bullied by their fellow pupils and struggled to keep up with their lessons. After failing the first grade they felt humiliated by having to repeat it.

''They were always the butt of sick jokes at school,'' remembered Susie, who later joined them in the first grade. ''Janie has a mole on her head and the other children used to tease them, saying that it was both of their brains. It upset them a lot.''

Their home life was even worse. Their stepfather regularly beat the children when he came home at night and Susie and the twins had to rely on each other to survive his abuse.

At the age of fifteen Janie and Genie both became pregnant and left school at the end of the eighth grade. When the fathers disappeared, the desperate twins married other men but were incapable of bringing up their children, who had to be raised by other family members.

By their early twenties both twins were divorced and struggling to get by. In desperation Genie decided to start a new life, moving to Germany. But she fared no better across the Atlantic and suffered a nervous breakdown. Incredibly, Janie felt her twin sister's pain and anguish even though she was thousands of miles away.

"It was amazing," said Susie Cerullo. "Before anyone knew there was something wrong with Genie, Janie knew exactly what was happening. Their hearts were together and even though one was in Germany the other could feel her pain in America."

When Genie returned to the States she settled in the small town of Newport, on the borders of Ohio and West Virginia. Over the next few years she married and had several more children, who would never live with her.

Sixty miles away, in Hamilton, Janie's life was also in tatters. Like her twin she too had her three children taken away from her and was fighting an uphill battle to survive. During these difficult times in their thirties the twins would both attempt suicide on several occasions.

According to Susie Cerullo there was a history of mental illness in the family and their paternal grandmother was committed indefinitely to a state mental hospital in Bethlehem, Pennsylvania.

In 1992 Genie's son Sam was murdered during a car chase when his Camaro was run off the road by a gang after an argument in a bar over a bet on a pool game. The gang was arrested and a heartbroken Genie sat tearfully through a long trial, seeing the killers receive a minimum custodial sentence and a slap on the wrist.

"That really finished my sister off," said Cerullo. "She became very depressed and all she wanted to do was take those pills and go to sleep. She went all the way down and her spirit died with her son."

Over the next three years the twins had to cope with the deaths of their real father, a niece and a nephew. Genie increasingly turned to alcohol and pills to blot out her troubles.

In an uncanny mirror-image of her twin, Janie's life had also spiraled out of control. In 1993 she attempted suicide and was committed to a Virginia hospital and diagnosed as suffering from several personality disorders, including depression and schizophrenia.

On her release Janie seemed much improved after her treatment but her twin sister was falling even deeper into mental illness, which was exacerbated when her husband walked out.

By September 1996 Janie had became so

concerned about Genie that she insisted she temporarily move into her apartment at 933 Main Street, Hamilton, so she could look after her. But although Janie did her best to help, Genie was inconsolable and became obsessed with death.

Every night the twins took pills and drank into the early hours as they read the Bible together and debated suicide being a mortal sin in the Catholic Church. Genie was tortured by her religious faith and feared being condemned to purgatory if she died by her own hands.

One night she weakened and took an overdose of pills and had to be rushed to the hospital. On her release she vowed to try again, saying that she wouldn't fail the next time. Frantic with worry about her twin sister, Janie began to consider killing her so she could go to heaven and find everlasting peace.

A few days later she had made up her mind, telling a friend, Tim Humphrey, that she was going to take a butcher's knife and stick it through Genie's heart.

"I'm going to put my sister out of her misery," she told Humphrey. "I don't care what they do to me."

But Humphrey didn't take her seriously and thought she was joking.

On Sunday, September 29th, the twins got up late and took a walk to buy groceries. It was late afternoon on a sunny fall day but the twins hardly noticed as they walked past a stream of happy, smiling people on their way home from church.

Both sisters had made a silent pact that morning that murder was the only way out of their predicament. They had never needed words to communicate and their decision, though unspoken, had given them an inner peace and made them feel closer than ever.

It was late afternoon when they returned to Janie's apartment and closed the front door behind them. Once inside Genie put on her favorite blues music while Janie went into the kitchen to fetch a bottle of whisky and some muscle relaxants. She knew exactly what she had to do and she was ready.

At six o'clock a Hamilton police dispatcher received a 911 alarm call from a disoriented-sounding woman who refused to give her name.

"Yes. I just set a fire to a house," she calmly told the astonished dispatcher. "It's 933. It's burning."

When the police operator asked her to repeat herself, the caller matter-of-factly replied, "I just said I just set fire to a house."

"You just set fire to a house?"

"Yes."

"At 933 Main Street?"

"Yes."

"Is that an apartment in the back?"

"I don't know."

"You don't know where you're at? Is it a house?"

"I set a fire!"

"Did you put it out?"

"Nope."

"Did you do it on purpose?"

"She's lying on the couch."

"Who's lying on the couch?"

"My sister."

When the dispatcher asked the woman again if she had set the fire deliberately or accidentally, she hung up.

By the time the Hamilton Fire Department arrived at the burning house, Janie Deitriech was already on her way to the hospital, having been rescued by a neighbor. Firemen rushed in to find the remains of Genie's body lying on a couch in the living room.

An hour later in the emergency room at Fort Hamilton–Hughes Memorial Hospital, Janie was arrested for arson and the murder of her twin sister.

From her emergency room bed Janie told Detective James Nugent that she could not recall how the fire started or even how she got out of her burning home. She claimed to have blacked out when the fire started.

Janie tearfully told the detective that she was sitting at her living room table reading the Bible and listening to music when she discovered the fire.

"She related her sister Genie was depressed because her husband had left her three weeks ago and [was] depressed over the death of her son several years ago," Detective Nugent would later testify at a preliminary murder hearing.

"She said they discussed suicide but if [Genie] did that she wouldn't get to heaven. But if she died another way she would get to heaven. She said that if her sister asked her to kill her, she would do that. She said if Genie wanted her to do it, she would kill her. She loved her sister *that* much."

The following day Janie was taken to the Butler County Jail and held in lieu of $100,000 bond to await trial on charges of aggravated murder and aggravated arson. She pleaded not guilty by reason of insanity.

But just three months later, while Janie was behind bars, tragedy struck the family again when the twins' eighteen-year-old nephew, Grant Cassidy, drowned in a Miami river after a police chase. The handsome, popular high school senior had become very depressed after his aunt's murder and had to change schools after classmates taunted him about it.

"It was yet another terrible tragedy for our family," said Susie Cerullo. "Grant froze to death in the river, trying to save his cousin who was running away from the police. There seemed to be a curse on us all."

*   *   *

On Wednesday, February 26, 1997, Janie Dei-triech pleaded guilty to the lesser charges of involuntary manslaughter of her sister and aggravated arson. In an emotionally dramatic hearing at Butler County Common Pleas Court, Janie's sister Susie Cerullo and other family members begged the judge to show mercy.

Entering the courtroom in handcuffs and leg shackles and wearing an orange prison uniform, Janie constantly broke down in tears as the court heard how she had deliberately started the fire that killed her sister.

"Janie and Genie were a pair," said her defense lawyer, Clayton Napier. "They were simpatico in the sense that they suffered from the same debilitating depression. I don't think I've ever seen anybody who led as shattered a life as this person. And Genie was at the point where she basically tried to sleep her life away."

The court heard that Janie had been physically and sexually abused as a child and recently diagnosed as suffering from schizophrenia, various personality disorders, chronic pain syndrome and major depression. But a court-appointed psychiatrist said that Janie was not legally insane when she set fire to her apartment.

The emotional climax of the hearing came when Susie Cerullo addressed Judge Michael Sage and her sister Janie collapsed in tears, forcing a five-minute recess so she could compose herself.

"Genie and Janie were very close," their sister told the judge, adding that Janie was acting purely out of love in killing their sister. "Whatever Janie did that night she did to help her sister. There was a deep closeness between them that no one else can ever understand."

Sentencing Janie to seven years in prison for each of the two charges, sentences to run concurrently, Judge Sage said that it was a particularly difficult judgment for him.

"I have tremendous sympathy for you and your family," he told a tearful Janie. "I certainly don't enjoy imposing a sentence in a case such as this, where mental illness played such a large part. But life is precious. Even though you and your sister had a very difficult life, life should be preserved at all costs. We can't have a society where people take the responsibility for ending other people's lives."